Alexander Vasiliev

CHILDREN'S FASHION
OF THE RUSSIAN EMPIRE

Glagoslav Publications

CHILDREN'S FASHION
OF THE RUSSIAN EMPIRE

by Alexander Vasiliev

Translated by James Womack

© 2014 Glagoslav Publications, United Kingdom

Glagoslav Publications Ltd
88-90 Hatton Garden
EC1N 8PN London
United Kingdom

www.glagoslav.com

ISBN 978-1-78384-030-4

A catalogue record for this book is available from the British Library.

Contents

Author's note

You hold in your hands a book that is unique in Russia. It is dedicated to children's fashion and clothing from the cities of the Russian empire between the 1860s and the 1910s. Why this timeframe in particular? Well may you ask. The truth is that photographic *cartes de visite* — photographs glued onto small pieces of card — only appeared in Russia at the end of the 1850s during the reign of the Emperor Alexander II. This gives us the starting point for our story. Gathering together a large collection of photographs of children, we deliberately end our book in 1917, a time of governmental upheaval and revolution, the conclusion to the era of Old Russia.

I have been collecting old photographs for more than thirty-five years, and in my collection, which makes up a large part of the Alexander Vasiliev Fund, there are more than 10,000 photographs to some degree connected with fashion. This book is simply the next step in the publication of this valuable archival material, but at the same time it is also change to: my first large-scale illustrated edition in English with Glagoslav Publications, and also the first book exclusively devoted to children's fashion.

It is usual to speak a lot about children nowadays. All parents, and especially mothers, worry about how to bring up their children, how to develop their tastes, their sense of national identity, their behaviour, their education and their culture. If this is the case with you, then take a look at this book. Perhaps when you have read it through and looked closely at all the photographs, you will have fewer questions.

Throughout the history of Imperial Russia, children's clothing, as you shall see, had great importance as one of the chief elements in an individual's upbringing. Of course, fashions changed, but there existed in those days — alas, a tradition that has now practically fallen away — a form of dress specifically for children, very different from that of adults in its cut, its length, its fabric and its accessories. The crinolines that were fashionable in the 1850s and 1860s gave way in the 1870s to bustles, which were in their turn followed by flounced dresses with gigot sleeves; Fauntleroy and sailor suits were current for boys in the 1890s, but by the 1900s and 1910s *style moderne* had taken complete control of the child's wardrobe.

Judging from the many surviving photographs, the standard of living among the gentry, the urban bourgeoisie and the petty bourgeoisie was high in Russia. All of the children seem happy, well fed and well cared for; their hair is cut, curled and pinned up, their clothes and stockings are clean, and their shoes are in good condition. I am sure that fashions of the past taught children how to be neat, how to look after their elegant clothing, to respect the handiwork of the seamstresses and furriers, tailors and cobblers who had made their clothing. To begin with, all children's clothing in the past was made by hand, whether it was made at home or bought elsewhere. In Russia's larger cities there were a number of ateliers and workshops that specialised exclusively in children's clothing. The largest collection of such vintage clothing in Russia is housed in the State Historical Museum. According to their recently published catalogue for the exhibition *Children's Clothing from the Eighteenth Century to the First Quarter of the Twentieth*, the most famous workshops which specialised in this form of production were A. Vakhovskaya's Children's World, Madame Zina's *Studio and Showroom for Children's Suits and Dresses*, M.P. Mezentsev's *Children's Dresses*, M. Koletis's *Showroom for Children's Clothing*, T.A. Yezhikova's *Children's Outfitters* and the *Children's Education* showroom, amongst others. Most of the main workshops in Moscow, Saint Petersburg, Riga, Warsaw and Kiev created clothing not just for adults, but for children as well.

Aside from fashionable ready-made clothes, 'folk' clothing was very popular in pre-Revolutionary Russia. In general, children took on their understanding of national character from their nurse, who would always be dressed in her sleeveless *sarafan* dress and her *kokoshnik* — her head-dress — and they would gladly wear homemade *kosovorotki, sarafanchiki, armyachki* and *cherkeski* (peasant shirts, *sarafans*, thick woollen overcoats, and Georgian-style long coats). They were not laughed at for this, nor did they feel uncomfortable, as children would nowadays, when they more often than not only think about American clothes and shoes and games. As can be seen from the photographs, these children were surrounded by extremely attractive, aesthetically pleasing toys — dolls, toy horses, hoops and drums. These children also loved their pets. The children in our album are often accompanied by dogs, both large and small, and by cats. There is also a certain amount of information to be gleaned from these photographs about pre-Revolutionary demographics. The type of family which is described in these photographs is always 'complete', with a father and a mother, brothers and sisters: united, monolithic, kind.

It is a matter of sincere regret that not all of these photographs have the names of their subjects inscribed upon them. When the child's name is known, we have indicated it in the caption. I am sure that this will help many of our readers discover the roots of their family and uncover previously lost family ties, as has already been the case thanks to the photographs reproduced in my previous books. If it is the case that you recognise any of the faces in this book, I ask you to get in touch with the publisher, or else with me via my personal website, www.vassiliev.com, and we will carry out the necessary changes to future editions of this book.

To conclude, I would like to thank my Russian publisher Pavel Podkosov, Irina Seriogin from Alpina Non-Fiction, my sister Natalia Tolkunova, who edited the Russian text, and my literary secretary, Vasili Snegovsky, who helped me caption the photographs; and my British publishing house Glagoslav Publications for bringing this book to the English reader. I hope that you will find this book necessary and useful, and I wish you the very best of times, reading it and looking at the images.

The 1860s

In the 1860s, children's clothing in Russia largely followed the general trends which came from Paris. Up until the age of five, boys' and girls' clothing had certain insignificant differences. Both sexes wore smocks over short skirts and culottes. The custom was to dress brother and sister in the same fashion.

For the whole of the decade, many children's costumes were made out of Scottish tartan fabric, with its chequered pattern. Taffeta, organdie, tarlatan and barège were also popular. The preference was largely for white clothes. 'For girls aged between five and six, nothing can be better than a white dress, even in winter, both for paying visits and for staying at home. Add to it a wide sash, which can be light blue, pink, violet or cherry-red, and tie it behind them with a large trailing bow. The bodice can be left open with a muslin chemise underneath, and boots of the same colour as the sash should be worn. Trousers and skirts should be in the English style and pleated. A white dress is not a wasted investment, as many mothers think. Quite the contrary, it has a great advantage: as it needs to be regularly changed, it can always be clean and new, and never goes out of fashion. With two white dresses, a child will always be well-dressed', the magazine *Fashion House* wrote. Other popular colours were pink, beige, black, grey and 'gooseberry'.

Girls, in imitation of adult fashions, still wore little crinolines and it was for this reason that they preferred to wear velvet cloaks, or shawls with fur collars, over their clothes. They also wore cashmere or velvet overcoats with details picked out in venice lace, a very popular fashion in those years. The Ivanova sisters from Saint Petersburg specialised in making children's overcoats.

Russian national imagery was very clearly displayed in boys' clothes. 'Most boys are dressed in the Russian style — this style in shirts and underclothing is very well known,' *Fashion House* wrote. Shirts were often trimmed with black braid to suggest Russian stitching. The unheard-of wave of interest in national costume even made it as far as Paris, where aspects of Russian national costume appeared in children's fashions, especially in the kind of braiding known as 'Russian stitch', usually created with black thread. In these years the French fashion press often mentioned 'Russian' shoes for children, or 'Russian fur collars' and 'Russian shirts'.

Towards the end of the decade, the fashion in decoration for boy's clothing gradually moved away from sewn ornament or appliqué; shirts began to be decorated with ribbons or else had their borders embroidered with rep. But the fashion for Russian-style *kosovorotki* or Algerian zouave-style jackets, as well as the wide 'coachman-style' trousers, still retained its importance.

The other fashionable daily garment for boys was the Breton jacket — a short jacket made from velvet, or else a shawl worn with knee-length trousers and a waistcoat. 'A little boy's clothes: grey or brown cashmere trousers, a shirt of the same colour with black embroidery, a sailor's straw hat with a black velvet band and a red ostrich feather,' was a description given by one observer of fashion at the time.

❖ Girl in formal dress. Photograph by
M. Konarsky. Novaya fotografiya Rossiskogo
obschestva liubitelej sadovodstva. Moscow.
1865.

❖ Girl in formal dress with ruche detail and
long trousers. Photograph by V. Ilmar.
Novgorod. 1866.

Girl from the Knyazev family in formal dress
❖ with an apron. Saint Petersburg. 1860s.

❖ Girl in formal weekend dress. Photograph
by G. Sachowicza. Warsaw. 1869.

G. SACHOWICZ   W WARSZAWIE

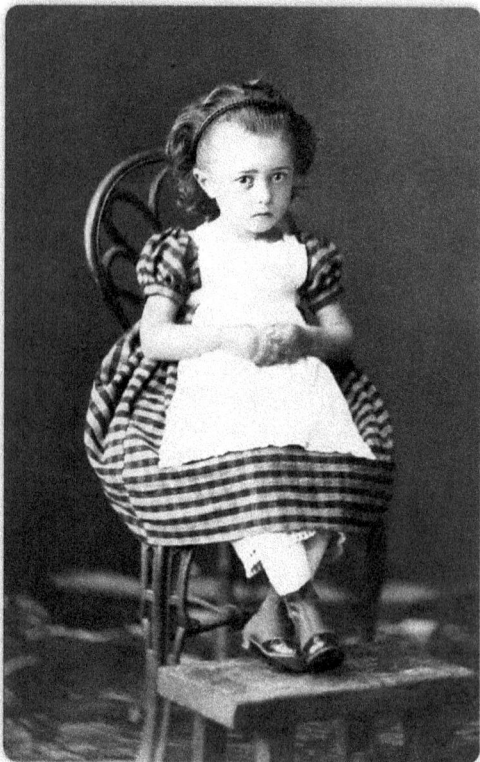

❖ Girl in inexpensive dress and 'Garibaldi'
outdoor jacket. Russia. 1867.

❖ Girl in weekend dress with ribbon detail.
Photograph by V. Kukushkin. Ivano-
Voznesensk. 1868.

❖ Girl in 'Balmoral-style' house dress with an
apron. Russia. 1865.

❖ Manya Girs in formal dress. Photograph by G.
Shteinberg. Saint Petersburg. 1867.

Girl in house dress. Photograph by
S. Novodereshkin. Zadonsk. 1869.

Girl in house dress. Photograph by the artist
Letunov. Moscow. 1864.

Two sisters in crinoline dresses, outdoor
jackets with fur trim, hats with feathers and
long trousers. Saint Petersburg. 1866.

Girl in outdoor dress with a pelerine,
decorated with a taffeta ribbon. Photograph
by Mebius on the Bolshaya Lubianka at
Mosolov's. Moscow. 1865.

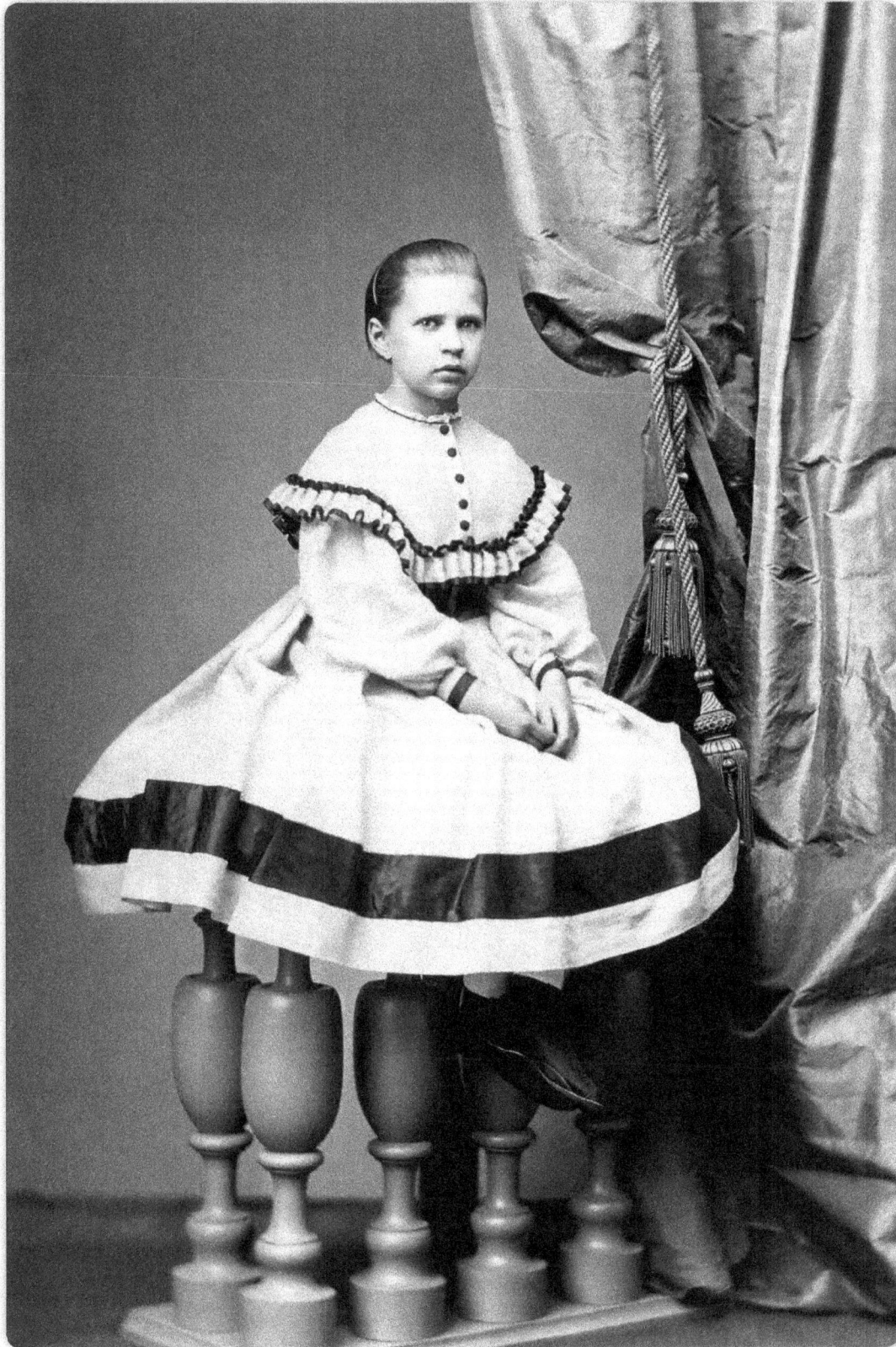

Yulia Vysotskaya in 'Russian' dress: embroidered blouse, velvet waistcoat, taffeta skirt, rope of artificial pearls. Russia. 1865.

Girl in striped house dress. Photograph by A. Luarsabov. 1869.

Girl in school uniform. Photograph by A. Schmidt. Kostroma. 1869.

Girl in taffeta outdoor dress with a belted crinoline and a cape. Russia. 1865.

❖ *Girl in 'Balmoral-style' dress wearing artificial pearl necklace. Saint Petersburg. 1866.*

❖ *Princess Baryatinskaya in outdoor dress with a crinoline and a velvet cape with openwork detail on the collar. Holding a hat with feathers. Photograph by Disderi & Co. Italy. 1860.*

❖ *Girl in formal outdoor dress with a crinoline and a Chantilly canezou. Russia. 1865.*

❖ *Girl in taffeta house dress. Saint Petersburg. 1869.*

❖ Girl in outdoor dress with a crinoline and
a black tulle headscarf, wearing a pearl
necklace. Russia. 1861.

❖ Girl with cape. Photograph by. G. Shteinberg.
Saint Petersburg. 1868. .

❖ Girl in school uniform with an apron, holding
a photograph album. Saint Petersburg. 1866.

❖ Boy in formal costume with rep detail.
Photograph by the artist E. Bollinger. Saint
Petersburg. 1867.

E. BOLLINGER PHOT.

Boy in 'Balmoral' fabric shirt with a wide belt. Moscow. 1860s.

Boy in three piece suit. Photograph by S.V. Rylov. Moscow. 1865.

Boy in everyday costume: zouave jacket with ribbon detail and knee britches. Photograph by Bishevsky. Vyatka. 1863.

Kolya Zarudny in a shirt with a belt and a turndown collar and 'coachman' trousers, tucked into morocco-leather boots. Russia. 1860s.

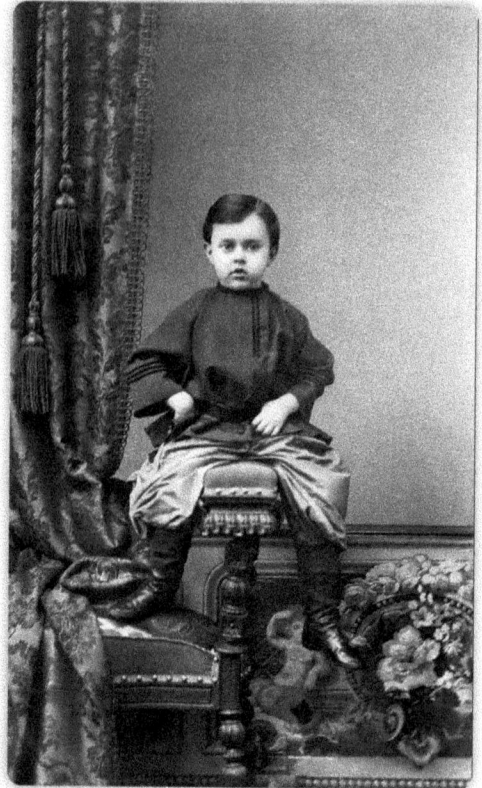

Художн. Н.Доссъ.

❧ Boy in cloth jacket. Photograph by N. Doss. Moscow. 1865.

❧ Boy in red kosovorotka and light-coloured 'coachman' trousers, tucked into morocco-leather boots. 1860s.

❧ Boy from the Chertkov family in kosovorotka and light-coloured 'coachman' trousers, tucked into morocco-leather boots. Russia. 1860.

◆ Boy in kosovorotka and 'coachman' trousers,
tucked into morocco-leather boots. Russia.
1860.

◆ Boy in stylised chequered kosovorotka and
wide 'coachman' trousers. Photograph by E.
Humblot. Dresden. 1866.

Boy in school uniform. Tula. 1860.

JAN MIECZKOWSKI   W WARSZAWIE

Boy in formal velvet outfit 'à la Van Dyck'. Girl in dress, the lower half of which is in Balmoral-style fabric. Russia. 1864.

Mother and daughter. Daughter in a formal outdoor outfit: a wave-hemmed skirt with a crinoline with ribbon detail, and a jacket the same. Photograph by J. Mieczkowski. Warsaw. 1867.

Family portrait. Photograph by the artist Zemlyansky. 1861.

ФОТОГРАФЪ   КОНОВАЛОВЪ.

❧ Boy in sailor suit with ribbon detail. Girl in formal dress with velvet ribbon detail. Photograph by P. Barth. Dorpat. 1865.

❧ The Adamovich children. Girl in formal weekend dress. Boy in stylised kosovorotka with soutache detail. Photograph by F.P. Konovalov. Kronstadt. 1868.

❧ Family portrait. Mother and two daughters in house dresses with crinolines and round-hemmed boleros. Photograph by W. Lauffert. Russia. 1862.

Family portrait. Girls in outdoor dresses with crinolines. Russia. 1863.

Brother and sister in formal weekend outfits. Photograph by Gebruder Winter. Prague. 1862.

Mother and son. Boy in Russian-style shirt. Photograph by W. Lauffert. Russia. 1868.

Girl from the Nikiforov family in double-breasted velvet overcoat with soutache detail on the collar and cuffs, holding an astrakhan muff. Russia. C.1865..

The 1870s

At the start of the 1870s fashion underwent a sea change. For the first half of the decade Paris gave the lead, as before, and Charles Worth's 1869 invention of the bustle — a heavy gathering of drapery behind the skirt — completely changed women's silhouettes and became universally popular, in Russia as well. The long epoch of wide skirts with crinolines had come to an end.

Children's clothing, like women's, underwent a significant change in the 1870s. With the disappearance of the crinoline, the fashion in children's dresses also changed — a narrow silhouette with drapery became de rigueur. In the first half of the 1870s, judging from the photographs of that period, children's fashion tended to copy that of adults. Little girls often were dressed in hand-me-downs from their older sisters, or even from their mothers. The dresses were pleated, and frills and festoons were also popular. Fabric was gathered behind the skirt, or else a large bow was placed there in imitation of the bustle. The influence of the English queen Victoria meant that tartan remained an important element in clothing design. Girls wore formal tartan dresses in the 'Balmoral' style, and often decorated them with velvet sashes. Younger girls wore pantaloons that could be seen underneath their skirts (skirts for the younger girls had very high hemlines). As the girls grew older, so their dresses lengthened, and at the age of sixteen a girl would be given her first long dress.

In the second half of the 1870s, girls began to wear dresses with very low waists, often emphasised by a rep or faille sash. This fashion turned out to be very hard-wearing and survived for the next forty years. The materials chosen for children's outfits were more often than not the ones that were easy to clean: calico, piqué, wool. Silk was in general used for more formal clothing. The available choice of materials widened considerably — the reign of Alexander II saw the country undergo a manufacturing revolution, including in its manufacture of textiles, as a result of which the Russian production of fabrics increased threefold.

In this decade, one novelty in particular was introduced into children's fashion — English outerwear. In particular, the double-breasted Ulster jacket with a pleated back (worn by both boys and girls), and comfortable clothing for rainy weather: hooded waterproof coats. In the winter, girls would wear cotton overcoats, headscarves and muffs. Many items were made from fur.

Popular clothing for boys included sailor suits with turndown collars. Also, velvet outfits à la Lord Fauntleroy — named after the protagonist of Frances Hodgson Burnett's children's novel *Little Lord Fauntleroy* — became popular. This was how *Fashion World* described the outfit: 'This black velvet outfit consists of trousers and a shirt, buttoned together, with the buttons concealed under a five-centimetre-wide belt. The collar and cuffs are made of thin cloth. Red stockings and high leather shoes.' This outfit stayed in fashion until the 1920s. As for headgear, boaters and Scottish pilot-style straw hats were widespread.

Girl in infant's summer clothing. Russia. 1870.

Girl in formal dress. Photograph by K.A. Fisher. Orenburg. 1878.

Girl in formal light wool weekend dress with venice lace and rep ribbon details. Photograph by P.G. Tikhonov. Vyatka. 1872.

Girl in formal house dress with frill and ruche detail. Photograph by A. Schönfeld. Saint Petersburg. 1870.

Portrait Album
ШЕНФЕЛЬДЪ   SCHÖNFELD
Невскій № 62 С. Петербургъ.   Newsky № 62, St Petersbourg.

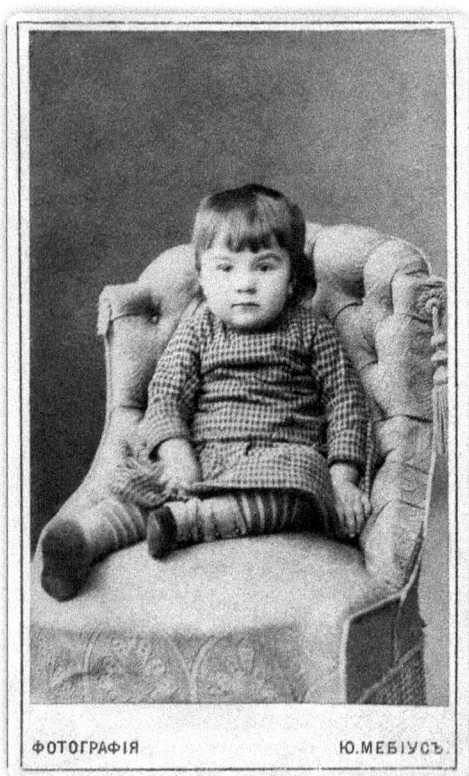

ФОТОГРАФІЯ   Ю.МЕБІУСЪ.

Girl in chequered woollen house dress. Photograph by Iu. Mebius. Moscow. 1870.

Girl in calico house dress. Photograph by Fr. De Mezer. Kiev. 1878.

Girl in double-breasted house dress. Russia. 1879.

Girl in chequered outdoor dress with lace ruche detail, soutache and taffeta ribbons. Photograph by S.M. Simonov. Moscow. 1876.

Фотогр. Симоновъ.

Г. Ф. ПРИГОЖАГО.

ФОТОГРАФІИ   Н. С. КАЗМИНА.

Dina Chernova in formal dress with ruche and frill detail. Photograph by F. Prigozhev. Kursk. 1872.

Girl in formal woollen weekend dress with ruche detail. Russia. 1873.

Girl in formal dress. Photograph by. G. Shteinberg. Saint Petersburg. 1870.

Girl in formal dress with waved hem and inkle detail. Photograph by. G. Shteinberg. Saint Petersburg. 1872.

✤ Girl in formal dress with frill and ruche detail. Russia. 1873.

✤ Girl in formal dress with ruche and plissé detail. Photograph by V.S. Doskin. Kharkov. 1874.

✤ Girl in striped mid-season outdoor dress. Russia. 1875.

✤ Girl in visiting dress with button detail. Photograph by J. Antonopoulo. Odessa. 1878.

Girl in school uniform with apron. Omsk. 1875.

Girl in striped taffeta dress. Photograph by V. Bebin. Kazan. 1878.

Girl from the Menarsky family in low-waisted 'Balmoral' style house dress, with faille sash at the waist. Photograph by O. Tadovsky. Samara. 1879.

Girl in outdoor summer dress with ruche and frill detail. Photograph by K. Anderson. Saint Petersburg. 1878.

СПБ Петербур.Фотогр. Харьковъ.

ФОТОГРАФІЯ
ВЯЗМИТИНОЙ
ОРЕЛЪ.
КАРАЧЕВСКАЯ УЛИЦА.
СОБСТВЕННЫЙ ДОМЪ.

Zina Lirikova in chequered house dress with low waist and plissé detail. Photograph by Kharkov. Saint Petersburg. 1876.

Girl in Russian-style embroidered house dress. Photograph by Vyazmitina. Orel. 1878.

Two girls in formal dresses with ruche detail. Photograph by K. Anderson. Saint Petersburg. 1875.

Liuba Popova in mid-season outdoor dress. Photograph by Cherno-Ozerskaya. Kazan. 1873.

Фот. Черно озерская   въ Казани.

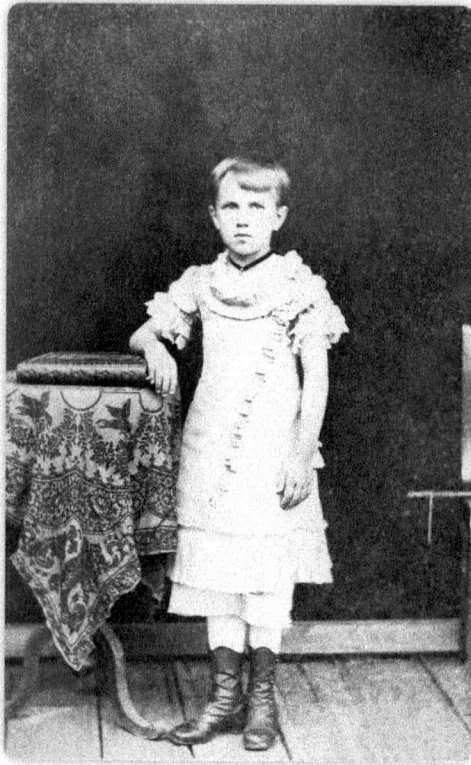

Girl in formal dress with ruche and frill detail.
Photograph by Murashev. Velikiye Luki.
1878.

Girl in mid-season outdoor dress with
plissé detail. Photograph by Daniel Nyblin.
Helsingfors. 1876.

Girl in house dress. Photograph by Robert
Borchardt. Riga. 1870.

Girl in school uniform with apron. Orenburg.
1878.

46

Славянская Фот.   въ Оренбургъ,

Girl in outdoor mid-season dress with ruche and plissé detail. Photograph by F. Konovalov. Kronstadt. 1879. .

Girl from noble family in expensive with ruche detail and decorative flower. Russia. 1878.

Girl in house dress with ruche detail. Moscow. 1870.

Girl in formal visiting dress with ruche and plissé detail. Photograph by M. Konarsky. Moscow. 1878.

М. КОНАРСКІЙ   ВЪ МОСКВѢ,
КУЗНЕЦКІЙ МОСТЪ,   Д. СОЛОДОВНИКОВА.

Girl in taffeta outdoor dress with frill and ruche detail. Photograph by Ivanov. Yekaterinoslav. 1878.

Kaleriya in house dress with an apron, ruche detail. Barnaul. 1873.

Girl in school uniform. Photograph by I. Dyagovchenko. Moscow. 1873.

Girl in house dress. Photograph by R. Tile. Moscow. 1872.

ХУДОЖНИКЪ
Р.Тиле
ПРИДВОРНЫЙ ФОТОГРАФЪ
КУЗНЕЦКІЙ
МООТЪ 13.
МОСКВА

ФОТ. К. АНДЕРСОНЪ.

Girl in chequered house dress with high waist. Photograph by K.F. Felbinger. Saint Petersburg. 1870–1875. .

Two girls in school uniform with plissé detail and white aprons. Photograph by N. Okolov. Minsk. 1876.

Girl in house dress with rep sash detail. Photograph by K. Anderson. Saint Petersburg. 1875.

Maria Sarochenkova in taffeta outdoor dress with festoon and frill detail. Photograph by E. Bollinger. Saint Petersburg. 1876.

Girl in chequered house dress with frill detail. Russia. 1877.

Girl in outdoor dress with ruche and frill detail. Photograph by I. Terekhov. Yekaterinburg. 1875.

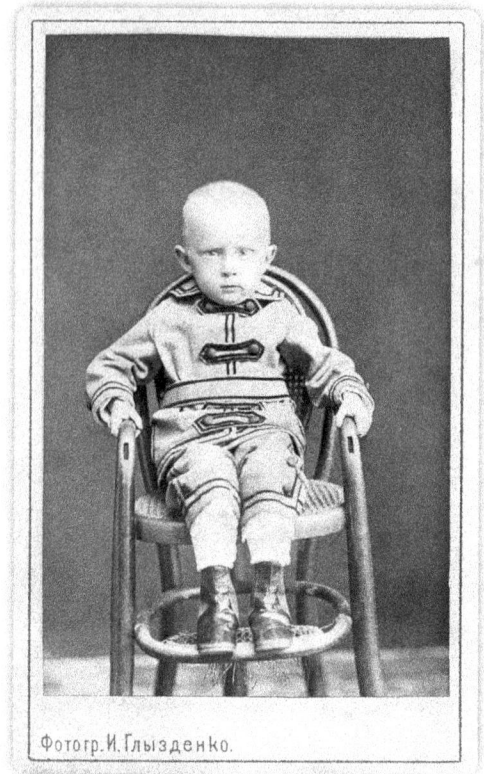

Фотогр.И.Глызденко.

ФОТОГРАФІЯ   Л. ГЕНЦШЕЛЬ.

❧ Boy in armyaka and kosovorotka with an oar. Omsk. 1870.

❧ Maksim Durzenevsky in formal outfit with sailor's collar, inkle detail and decorative buttons. Photograph by I. Glyzdenko. Nizhny Novgorod. 1873.

❧ Boy in short velvet trousers. Photograph by L. Gentsshel. Saint Petersburg. 1870.

❧ Liosha Skorodumov in nightshirt with embroidered detail. Photograph by Iu. Mebius. Moscow. 1875.

ФОТОГРАФІЯ Ю. МЕБІУСА.

Boy in embroidered kosovorotka and short trousers. Photograph by K.F. Felbinger. Saint Petersburg. 1875.

Boy in black velvet outfit. Photograph by M.A. Vyatkin. Kazan. 1873.

Boy in kosovorotka and 'coachman' trousers. Melitopol. 1876.

Boy in dark blue woollen sailor suit with white ribbon detail. Photograph by V. Lapre. Russia. 1874.

❧ Boy in house outfit. Photograph by A.Bakh. Samara. 1870.

❧ Boys in school uniform. Photograph by I. Glyzdenko. Ivano-Voznesensk. 1877.

❧ Boy in dark wool riding outfit, velvet waistcoat, Scottish stockings and buttoned half boots. Photograph by 'Leon'. Saint Petersburg. 1877.

❧ Boys from the Agureev family in black velvet outfits à la Lord Fauntleroy. Photograph by K.A. Shapiro. Saint Petersburg. 1878.

BERGAMASCO.PHOT.

ФОТОГРАФІЯ   ЕРМОЛИНА.

❖ *Boy from the Nikiforov family in visiting outfit. Photograph by Bergamasco. Saint Petersburg. 1870s.*

❖ *Boy in house outfit. Photograph by V.A. Gassi. Kazan. 1875.*

❖ *Boy in cadet uniform. Photograph by N.A. Yermolin. Saint Petersburg. 1875.*

❖ *Boys in cadet uniform. Russia. 1870.*

❖ Two brothers. One in school uniform, the other in kosovorotka and 'coachman' trousers, tucked into morocco-leather boots. Photograph by I.S. Byalobrzhevsky. Zhitomir. 1871.

❖ Boy in jacket and kosovorotka. Photograph by M.A. Vyatkin. Kazan. 1870.

❖ Sister with two brothers. Boys in formal outfits à la Lord Fauntleroy with decorative button detail. Girl in low-waisted 'Balmoral' style outdoor dress with frill detail. Russia. 1878.

❖ Girls in woollen double-breasted overcoats with sailor collars. Photograph by W. Lauffert. Saint Petersburg. 1870.

PHOTOGRAPHIE   W. LAUFFERT.

Brother and sister. Boy in formal outfit with braid detail. Girl in formal dress. Photograph by F. Vishnevsky. Moscow. 1872.

Father with son. Boy in black velvet outfit à la Lord Fauntleroy. Photograph by A. Ivanitsky. Belgorod. 1878.

Mother and daughter. Girl in formal dress. Photograph by. G. Shteinberg. Saint Petersburg. 1874.

Family portrait. Children in formal weekend outfits. Photograph by M. Moss. Russia. 1876.

Brother and sisters. Boy in black velvet outfit à la lord Fauntleroy with lace collar. Girls in formal velvet-fronted weekend dresses with ruche detail and decorative buttons. Photograph by A. German. Yaroslavl. 1879.

Mother and daughter. Girl in formal dress with frill detail. Russia. 1876.

Family portrait. Children in inexpensive weekend outfits. Photograph by H. Richter. Kishinev. 1875.

Volodya and Manya Belov in formal weekend outfits. Photograph by R. Beyer. Saint Petersburg. C.1870.

ФОТОГРАФІЯ ЛИНДСТРЕМА

Boy in outdoor outfit with sailor collar, Scottish stockings and buttoned half-boots. Girl in house dress with festoon detail. Photograph by Cherno-Ozerskaya. Kazan. 1873.

Mother and daughter. Girl in formal dress. Photograph by A. German. Yaroslavl. 1878.

Family portrait. Boy in outdoor outfit with turndown collar à la Lord Fauntleroy. Girl in formal outdoor dress with plissé detail. Photograph by K. Lindström. Saint Petersburg. 1878.

Дмитріевъ   Псковъ.

Фот.Страхова.   въ Москвѣ.

Mother with children. Girl in taffeta outdoor dress with turndown collar. Boy in outdoor outfit, holding a boater. Photograph by Dmitriev. Pskov. 1876.

Mother and daughter. Girl in outdoor dress with frill and ruche detail. Photograph by I. Strakhov. Moscow. 1878–1879.

Mother and daughter. Girl in outdoor dress with turndown collar and ruche and plissé detail. Photograph by H&F Kiepert. Mitau. 1876.

The 1880s

In the 1880s, children's fashion developed rapidly and influenced the shape of much adult clothing in the twentieth century. A lot of attention was paid to girls' clothing. The most popular item was the 'princess-style' low-waisted one-piece dress, finished with a pleated skirt, often decorated with lace and embroidered patterns. It is impossible not to see the fashionable silhouette of the 1920s in the cut of this clothing, short and low-waisted as it is. The colours of girls' dresses in this period were extremely modest. Many dresses were accessorised with scarfs tied at thigh level, hanging in pleats. Tartan remained popular. For girls aged between 10 and 12, outdoor clothes were fitted with short polonaises in imitation of the bustle, recalling French clothing of the 1770s.

Girls and adult women wore corsets, but doctors had already begun to speak out against the practice of lacing children, as they claimed it was bad for the health. According to the famous doctor Shtrats, barely five girls out of a hundred grew up healthy and beautiful after early corset use.

The influence of Russian national costume was particularly visible during the reign of Alexander III. Dresses were often embroidered with cross-stitch in Russian style, bright tambour-stitch lace was popular for the details of children's dresses. Russian and Ukrainian-style children's dresses were no rarity in the 1880s, especially in Slavophile circles. For girls, overclothing tended to take the form of a pardessus coat with Irish-made venice lace details crocheted on, in every possible shade of brown. Girls aged between 8 and 10 wore buclé cotton overcoats with a fur lining and incorporated hood.

Boys aged between 2 and 4 wore little dresses just like girls did, as they were considered more comfortable. Here is a description of one of them from the magazine *Paris Fashion* from 1880: 'The outfit is a shirt and a little skirt. The blouse is decorated, as is the skirt, with two rows of soutache embroidery. The whole is secured at the front with large bone buttons, and the final touch is a supportive band of faille ribbon.' Scottish costumes were very popular for boys: these consisted of a dress that imitated the traditional kilt, a tartan sash and a traditional Scottish velvet hat. Older children were dressed in thick cotton outfits, with dark blue velvet cardigans with gold buttons, and sailor hats. Three-piece velvet suits with lace collars à la Van Dyck were also popular.

Also in widespread use for boys during the 1880s were sailor suits, consisting of military jackets with pleats in the front and the back, trousers and a vest. These were often made of thick cotton and were decorated on the front with gold or silver embroidered anchors.

Also fashionable at this time were double-breasted jackets in velvet or chequered wool, with flaps over the pockets and turndown collars. For children aged between 9 and 11, one option was outfits consisting of short trousers, buttoned at the knee, a little single-breasted waistcoat with four buttons, and a short double-breasted jacket with a narrow turndown collar. All of these would have inkle detail at the borders.

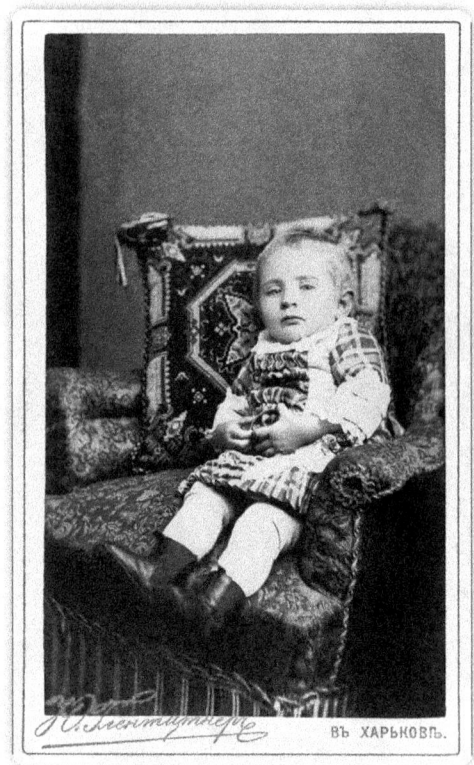

❖ Girl in house dress with ruche and lace detail. Photograph by I. Lvov. Moscow. 1880.

❖ Girl in formal 'Balmoral' style dress with ruche and plissé detail. Photograph by Iu. Glentitner. Kharkov. 1884.

❖ Girl in outdoor dress with turndown collar. Photograph by I. Lvov. Moscow. 1880.

❧ Two girls in house dresses with lace detail. Photograph by Iu. Shteinberg. Saint Petersburg. 1880.

❖ *Two girls in house dresses. Photograph by B.O. Gottlieb. Odessa. 1889.*

❖ *Girl in sailor-style outdoor dress. Photograph by Fedosev. Simbirsk. 1887.*

Girl in outdoor dress with Russian-style embroidery. Photograph by N. Abrahamson. Saint Petersburg. 1887.

❖ *Girl in house dress with band tied behind. Poltava. 1880s.*

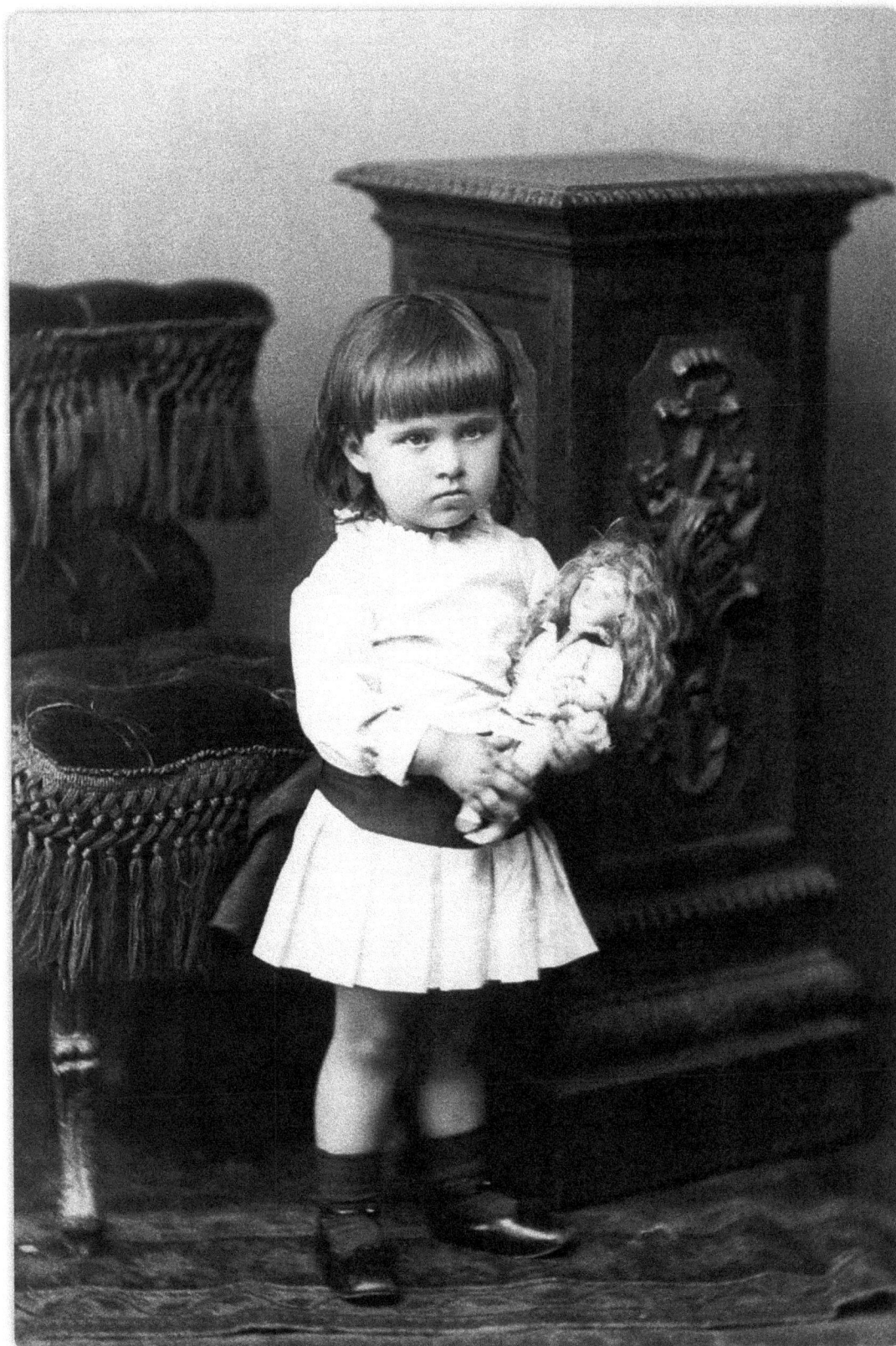

Girl with a hoop in outdoor dress with ruche and plissé detail. Photograph by V. Turnov. Moscow. 1882.

Girl in formal low-waisted outdoor dress with and a white lace pelerine. Photograph by T. Mitreiter. Moscow. 1885.

Two sisters in inexpensive outdoor dresses. Moscow. 1880.

Girl in silk visiting dress with lace detail on the lower skirts. Photograph by Scherer and Nabholz. Moscow. 1881.

SCHERER, NABHOLZ et Cie. a MOSCOU.

❧ Girl in 'Balmoral' style house dress. Photograph by Dorodnikova. Russia. 1881.

❧ Girl in formal dress with plissé and lace detail. Photograph by V. Vysotsky. Kiev. 1880.

❧ Girl in emboridered dress in 'pseudo-Russian' style. Theodosia. 1887.

❧ Girl in low-waisted house dress. Photograph by V. Yasvoin. Saint Petersburg. 1888.

80

БУЛГАКЪ И ОВЧАРЕНКО.   МОСКВА.

❖ Girl in visiting dress with velvet and plissé
   detail. Photograph by N.I. Borisov. Moscow.
   1880.

❖ Girl in formal dress with plissé detail.
   Photograph by Bulgak and Ovcharenko.
   Moscow. 1880.

   Girl in house dress. Photograph by
❖ K.A. Shapiro. Saint Petersburg. 1885.

❧ Girl in velvet house dress with lace collar.
   Photograph by Iu. Mebius. Russia. 1880s.

❦ *Girls in inexpensive house dresses. Photograph by L. Clüver. Saint Petersburg. 1880.*

❦ *Girl in house dress with velvet cuffs, belt and collar. Photograph by Fr. De Mezer. Kiev. 1887.*

❦ *Girl in house dress. Photograph by T. Mitreiter. Moscow. 1885.*

❦ *Girls in visiting dresses. Photograph by V. Taube. Saint Petersburg. 1887.*

84

Yulia Kozyreva in mid-season outdoor dress. Russia. 1881.

Girl in formal dress in 'Greenway' style with lace detail. Photograph by Fr. De Mezer. Kiev. 1889.

Girl in expensive formal house dress. Photograph by F. Orlov. Yalta. 1880.

ФОТОГРАФІЯ
Ф. ОРЛОВА   ВЪ ЯЛТѢ.

Girl in woollen English dress with sailor's collar. Photograph by Scherer and Nabholz. Moscow. 1886.

Girls in outdoor dresses with braided hussar-style detail. Photograph by R. Sobolev. Saint Petersburg. 1889.

Three girls in school uniform with aprons. Photograph by A Russov. Orel. 1880.

Four girls in school uniform. Yekaterinburg. 1880.

Vera and Katia in outdoor dresses. Photograph by F. Felbinger. Saint Petersburg. 1886.

Ф. ФЕЛЬБИНГЕРЪ

Петербургск. Стор. на Больш. пр. д. № 12.

F. FELBINGER

Petersburger Seite Grosser Prosp. H. № 12.

❧ *Boy in formal house outfit with ruche detail. Photograph by Fr. De Mezer. Kiev. 1887.*

❧ *Boy in sailor suit with white soutache detail. Photograph by A. Borel. Saint Petersburg. 1880.*

Boy in stylised sailor suit with anchors. Photograph by Zhorzh. Baku. 1887.

❧ *Boy in dark sailor suit with white inkle detail. Photograph by F. Czyz. Vilna. 1880.*

❧ Boy in sailor suit with ruche detail.
Photograph by A. Vasiliev. Samara. 1886.

❧ Boy in formal black velvet costume à la
Lord Fauntleroy: short trousers in C.XVII
style, lace detail underneath, and simple
jacket with lace collar. Photograph by
D.Ia. Nekrasov. Moscow. 1880.

Boy in kosovorotka and in dark velvet
trousers. Photograph by. V. Turnov. Moscow.
1885.

❧ Boy in outdoor outfit with sailor's collar.
Photograph by N. Grünberg. Saint
Petersburg. 1880.

Фотографія Грюнберга.

F. Schmitz   Riga.

Katya in velvet dress with ruche detail. Sasha in outfit of short trousers, fastened under the knee with three buttons, a little single-breasted waistcoat with four buttons and a short double-breasted jacket with a small turndown collar. Photograph by R. Beyer. Saint Petersburg. 1884.

Boy in light sailor suit. Voronezh. 1880.

Boy in house outfit: 'Russian' shirt, fastened with a belt, and short trousers. Photograph by F. Shmits. Riga. 1880.

Boy in outfit velvet à la Lord Fauntleroy with large silk ribbon-tie. Photograph by Bulgak and Ovcharenko. Moscow. 1880.

БУЛГАКЪ И ОВЧАРЕНКО.   МОСКВА.

❧ *Brother and sister. Girl in formal house dress with ruche and frill; boy in double-breasted jacket with turndown collar and short trousers, fastened under the knee with three buttons. Photograph by I.L. Lvov. Saint Petersburg. 1885.*

❧ *Boys in outdoor outfits. Photograph by A. Eikhenvald. Moscow. 1888.*

❧ *Boy in kosovorotka and trousers with Russian-style embroidery. Photograph by N. Grunberg. Saint Petersburg. 1882.*

❧ *Boy from the Tsigarelly family in light woollen Caucasian jacket, wearing a Caucasian hat (papakha) made from white sheepskin. Photograph by N. Kiselev. Pyatigorsk. 1880.*

Н. Киселевъ

КАВКАЗСКІЯ МИНЕР. ВОДЫ.

❖ Noble family with daughters. Girls in summer 'princess' style dresses, with ruche and embroidery detail. Photograph by N. Abrahamson. Saint Petersburg. 1884.

❖ Family portrait. Brothers in school uniform. Sisters in outdoor dresses with ruche detail. Moscow. 1880.

❧ Boy from the Tsigarelly family in light woollen Caucasian jacket, wearing a Caucasian hat (papakha) made from white sheepskin. Photograph by N. Kiselev. Pyatigorsk. 1880.

ХАРЬКОВЪ   ФОТ. СУЧКОВА.

St. Pétersbourg
Gr. Morskaïa H. Rentz & F. Schrader
· 30 ·

Boy and girl in outdoor outfits. Photograph by A Rents and F. Shrader. Stary Petergof. 1880.

Boy and girl. Boy in sailor outfit; Girl in formal dress with lace collar. Photograph by B. Makhovetsky. Saint Petersburg. 1886.

Family portrait. Boys in sailor outfits, girls in dresses with lace detail. Photograph by A. Reutov. Russia. 1880.

Family portrait. Boy in double-breasted straight-gut jacket and trousers. Photograph by. V. Turnov. Moscow. 1884.

Фотографія ✠ Трунова
ВЪ МОСКВѢ.

❖ Mother and son. Son in velvet outfit. Photograph by R.Iu. Tile. Moscow. 1889.

❖ Brother and sister. Boy in stylised kosovorotka and 'coachman' trousers; Girl in formal dress with lace detail. Photograph by R.Iu. Tile and Opits. Moscow. 1885.

❖ Brother with two sisters. Boy in sailor outfit, girls in formal dresses. Photograph by A. Borel. Saint Petersburg. 1883.

❖ O.I. Derzhavina with his granddaughters Shura and Katya. Girls in formal dresses in Russian style. Photograph by S.M. Simonov. Moscow. 1884.

❖ *Mother and son. Boy in dark velvet outfit à la Lord Fauntleroy with turndown lace collar. Photograph by F. Miller. Kiev. 1888.*

❖ *Brother and sister. Boy in school uniform; Girl in house dress with ruche detail. Photograph by P. Petrov. Novocherkassk. 1880.*

Brothers and sisters. Girls in black wool low-waisted house dresses, boys in straight-cut jackets and trousers. Photograph by N. Abrahamson. Saint Petersburg. 1885.

❖ *Mother with children. Boy in summer outfit with sailor's collar; girl in fashionable low-waisted summer dress with faille ribbon detail. Photograph by C. H. Bergamasco. Saint Petersburg. 1882.*

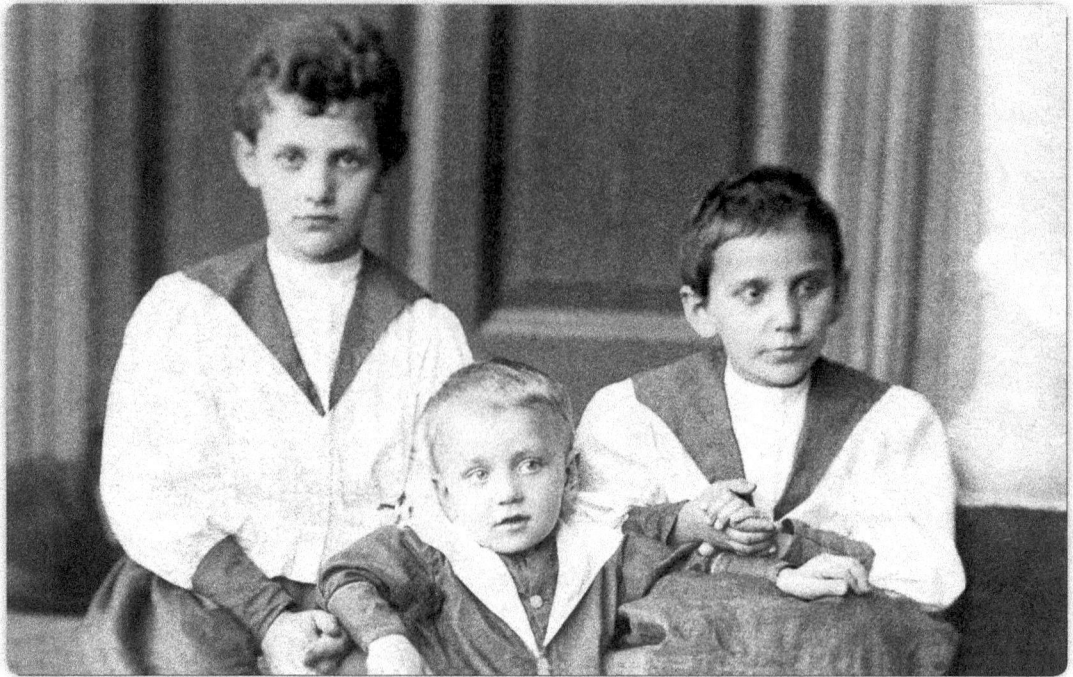

❧ Three brothers in summer outfits with sailor
collars. Saint Petersburg. 1889.

Mother and daughter. Girl in taffeta outdoor
dress. Photograph by E. Khorshev. Penza.
1884.

❧ Brother and sisters in mid-season outdoor
costumes. Warsaw. 1881.

Mother and daughter. Girl in knitted cotton overcoat and knitted hat. Photograph by P. Mukashev. Sumy. 1881.

Boy in double-breasted school overcoat with sheepskin collar. Photograph by Iu. Nikonovich. Saint Petersburg. 1880.

Brothers in half-length sheepskin overcoats. Photograph by N. Chesnokov. Saint Petersburg. 1888.

Girl in expensive marten-lined winter overcoat with fur-trimmed hat. Photograph by Vezenberg. Saint Petersburg. 1888.

Везенбергъ и К°.   С.Петербургъ.

The 1890s

Over the course of the next decade, changes in children's clothing became even more noticeable. Up until the age of four, boys wore little dresses with low waists, sometimes with embroidered Russian sidepieces. From the beginning of the 1890s boys began to wear dark cheviot trousers, and dark vests with light flannel sleeves. Particular affection was felt for the sailor suit with a large turndown collar. To this was often added a sailor hat with fleet ribbons.

Boys aged between 9 and 11 often wore untucked *kosorvorotki* with a leather belt, knee-length trousers and high boots.

Beginning in 1892, fashion magazines began to advertise cycling costumes. For boys these also often were reminiscent of sailor suits, with the addition of a low-crowned, wide-brimmed straw hat. Boys' shirts in the mid-1890s were made out of chequered fabric with broad sleeves, and wide ribbon-ties to finish. At the end of the 1890s, boys aged 3-10 began to wear knitted jersey outfits.

The fashion for young girls' dresses was very various in this period. Noting this, *The Ladies' Journal* wrote: 'As far as the modern *toilette* for young girls is concerned, we hasten to take note that so many changes have taken place that at the present day it is not in the least comparable with that of adults.' From birth up until the age of two girls would wear little dresses, normally made from fine white wool, already resembling children's fashions of the first half of the twentieth century. Five-year olds would wear dresses with plackets, short sleeves and a low cincture.

This low waist in girls' clothes would remain in fashion until the First World War, and would lead to the fashion in low-waisted clothes for adult women in the 1920s. Girls aged between seven and nine started to wear clothes that followed the natural line of the waist. Overcoats were made with leg-of-mutton sleeves, narrow down to the knee, giving a simple unwaisted silhouette. One novelty was blue-grey 'soldier' cloth: a jacket made out of this material would be decorated with a row of buttons. Children's overcoats were regularly made with velvet collars.

In order to bathe, girls aged between six and eight would wear combinations, normally of calico, with knee-length trousers. Older girls would wear bathing costumes, like adults did: dark blue, with a sailor's collar. In Russia, girls from good families carried little child-sized purses in bright running stitch, where they would keep their little handkerchiefs.

Russian-style fashion was still in vogue, as it was throughout the reign of Alexander III — children's clothes were often decorated with cross-stitch. Girls aged between four and six wore Russian-style dresses. These were like *kosovorotki*, without collars and with fabric overhanging the low-set waist. Russian-style dresses were also worn by girls aged between thirteen and fifteen, but they were longer, with a higher waist. Tartan, smooth cashmere, wool, muslin, batiste and velvet were popular fabrics for girls. Girls would often wear pinafores to protect their clothes from having to be washed too often.

N. J. Anouffrieff · St PÉTERSBOURG

❖ Child from the Permsky family in formal dress with lace detail. Russia. 1895.

❖ Klava Kasibalskaya in outdoor dress in sailor style, with white soutache detail. Photograph by A. Semenenko. Saint Petersburg. 1898.

❖ Child in short house dress. Photograph by A. Vasiliev. Samara. 1890.

❖ Girl in in formal dress with upright collar. Photograph by T. Serebrin. Voronezh. 1896.

114

Girl in house dress with embroidered apron and lace pelerine. Photograph by O. Rembrandt. Kazan. 1897.

Girl in formal dress with an apron. Photograph by. W. Zatorski. Kovno. 1895.

Girl in expensive formal dress, with ribbon detail. Photograph by I. Afanasiev. Kozlov. 1895.

Girl in house dress in Russian style, fastened with hooks. Photograph by V. Nikolaev. Tambov. 1895.

116

В. Николаевъ ТАМБОВЪ.

❖ Girl in formal dress with lace collar and cuffs, ruche detail. Photograph by M. Khripkov. Nizhny Novgorod. 1893.

❖ Polish children Yadviga and Maryla in formal weekend dresses. Photograph by F. Butkovsky. Vilna. 1899.

Girl in high-waisted dress. Russia. 1894.
❖

❖ Girl in formal dress with pelerine and lace inkle detail. Photograph by D. Zdobny. Saint Petersburg. 1895.

Rimma in taffeta outdoor dress with turndown sailor's collar. Russia. 1897.

Girl in school dress with apron. Photograph by M. Dmitriev. Nizhny Novgorod. 1898.

Girl in formal dress with lace collar. Photograph by G. Lazovsky. Kiev. 1895.

Lena in formal dress in sailor style. Photograph by A. Fedetsky. Kharkov. 1898.

A. Fedecki   АЛ   À Kharkoff.

◆ *Girl in Russian-style low-waisted house dress with upright collar. Photograph by G. Trunov. Moscow. 1890.*

◆ *Sisters Marusia and Asya in double-breasted woollen jackets with leg-of-mutton sleeves. Photograph by V. Taube. Saint Petersburg. 1895.*

Girl in ballgown. Photograph by M. Dubovik. Belaya Tserkov. 1890.

◆ *Girl in outdoor dress with ruche detail. Photograph by G. Trunov. Moscow. 1896.*

Г.В. ТРУНОВЪ   ПРИДВОРНЫЙ ФОТОГРАФЪ   МОСКВА.

Boy in formal costume with lace collar. Photograph by N. Ouzemsky. Kiev. 1895.

Young boy in house dress. Photograph by A. Pazetti. Saint Petersburg. 1890.

Boy in sailor suit. Photograph by E. Khorshev. Penza. 1895.

Boy in dark military jacket and cheviot trousers. Photograph by Bashinozhagyan. Novocherkassk. 1890.

Boy in formal costume à la Lord Fauntleroy.
Photograph by U. Ritter. Moscow. 1898.

Boy in outfit with Vologda lace collar.
Photograph by A. Leibin. Verny. 1897.

Boy in formal costume with shirt with
turndown collar and lace detail. Russia. 1894.

Boys from the Batkevich family in sailor
outfits with large turndown collars.
Photograph by D. Jucker. Kharkov. 1899.

Boy in sailor suit with large turndown collar. Saint Petersburg. 1890.

Boys in sailor outfits with largeu turndown collars and rep ribbon detail. Russia. 1893.

Boys from a wealthy family in formal outfits with lace detail. Photograph by Scherer and Nabholtz. Moscow. 1890.

Boy in smooth fabric chemise with puffed sleeves and large turndown collar, and knee-length britches. Photograph by Fr. Opits. Moscow. 1897.

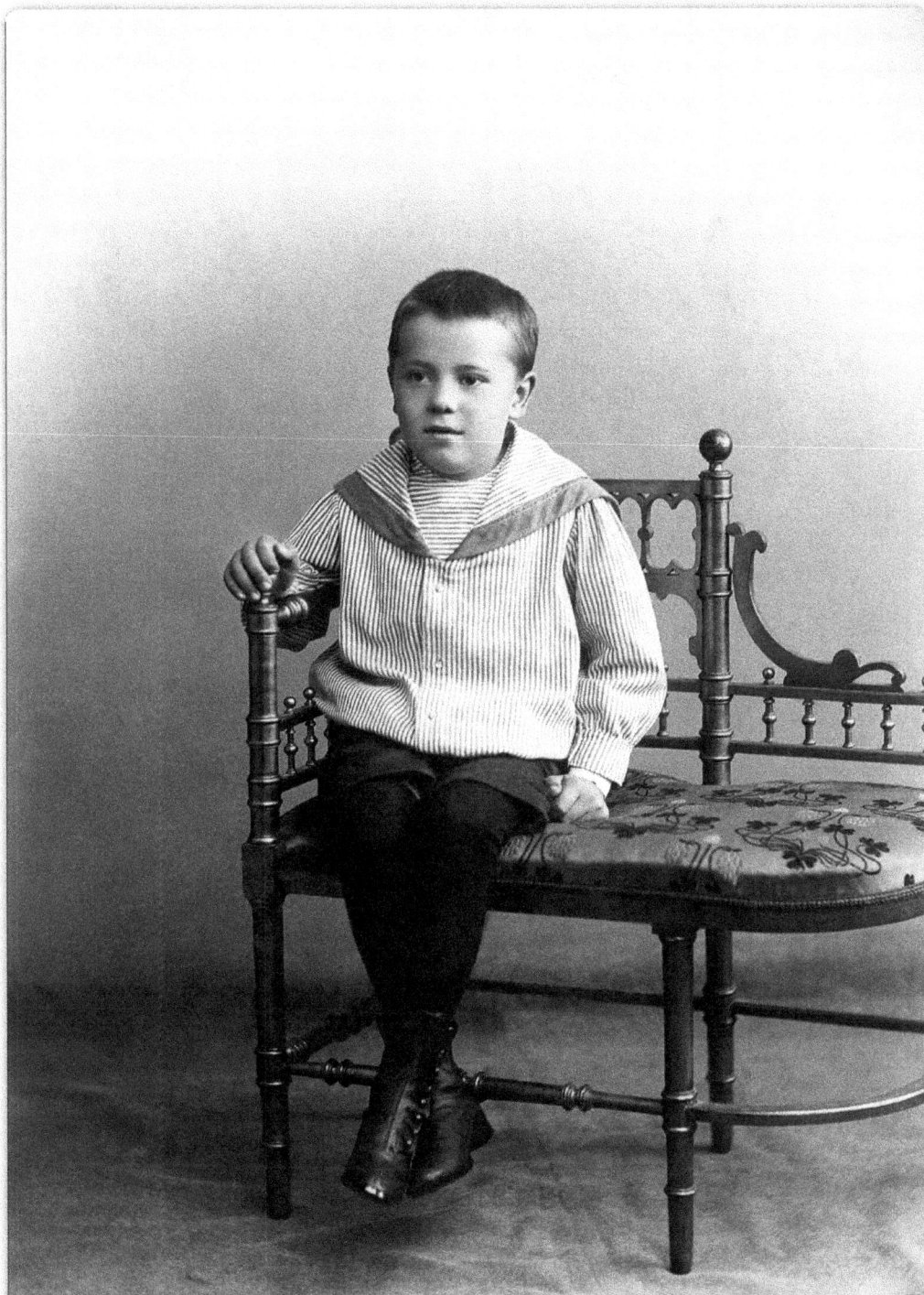

F. Spitz   Moscou.

Boys in outfits with turndown sailor's collars. Photograph by A. Serebrin. Voronezh. 1898.

Gymnazium pupil in uniform. Photograph by N. Iunyshev. Tomsk. 1890.

Cadet in uniform. Photograph by O. Rembrandt. Kazan. 1899.

Two brothers with mother and sister. Boys in outdoor outfits. Photograph by E. Ovcharenko. Moscow. 1895.

Е.Овчаренко ЕО въ Москвѣ.

Mother with sons. Boys in short knee-length trousers and striped chemises with sailor collars. Photograph by Scherer and Nabholz. Moscow. 1897.

Three sisters with their brother. The older children in in sailor outfits, the youngest girl in formal dress with lace detail. Russia. 1897.

Brother and sister. Boy in uniform; Girl in low-waisted dress with lace collar. Photograph by Serebrin. Vitebsk. 1895.

Mother and father with children, dressed in formal chequered fabric outfits. Photograph by E. Lyavdansky. Kovno. 1899.

E. Lawdanski À KOWNA

❧००५ Nurse with girl in white light wool dress
      and Russian headdress. Photograph by
      Petruschin-Svischev. Stavropol. 1897.

००❧ Mother and daughter. Girl in high-waisted
     house dress. Russia. 1895.

००%ॐ Nurse with boy in formal dress. Photograph
☙   by Francaise. Moscow. 1896.

❧ Brother with two sisters. Boy in Caucasian
   light wool jacket and white sheepskin
   papakha. Girls in dresses with ruche detail
   and lace. Photograph by Scherer and
   Nabholz. Moscow. 1892.

Photographie Francaise   Москва
                           СТОЛЕШНИКОВЪ ПЕР.
                           Д. ДЕ-КАРРІЕРЪ.

Scherer Nabholz & Cie. À Moscou.

❖ Mother and daughter in summer outdoor dresses with flounced sleeves. Photograph by Fr. Opitz. Moscow. 1896.

❖ Sister with three brothers.. Boys in cinched kosovorotki; girl in dress with purse and upright collar. Moscow. 1895.

❖ Brother and sister — Margarita and Georgii Morel. Margarita in chequered formal dress with collar and plissé detail. Georgii in dark wool blouse. Russia. 1898.

❖ Liza, Kolya, Volodya, Seriozha and Lenya Shlezinger. Boys in kosovorotki and narrow trousers; Girl in outdoor dress with rep ribbon detail and pelerine. Photograph by Scherer and Nabholz. Moscow. 1892.

Scherer Nabholz & Cie   À MOSCOU.

Brother and sister. Girl in low-waisted dress; boy in dark wool outfit with turndown collar. Photograph by S. Schmidt. Russia. 1889.

Brother and sister. Boy in jacket with turndown velvet collar. Photograph by A. Shkassa. Kharkov. 1898.

Brother and sister. Boy in blouse with decorative anchor and jacket with sailor's collar. Girl in formal dress with ribbon and lace detail. Photograph by S. Kurbatov. Moscow. 1895.

Brother with two sisters. Elder girl in house dress with frill detail, younger in school uniform with an apron. Boy in stylised kosovorotka and trousers tucked into high boots. Photograph by Yezersky. Kiev. 1890s.

Езерскій ❦ Кіевъ.

Mother and father with son. Boy in double-breasted overcoat with sheepskin collar and 'Russian' hat. Photograph by V. Mitkin. Yekaterinoslav. 1893.

Boy in 'swansdown' overcoat, hat and muff. Photograph by B. Bik. Samara. 1896.

Nina Baklushinskaya in woollen winter overcoat, with white sheepskin muff and fur collar. Photograph by V. Petukhov. Kamyshin. Late 1890s.

Boys in sheepskin overcoats and 'Russian' hats. Photograph by F. Rendel. Pinsk. First half of the 1890s.

В. Рендель   въ Пинскѣ.

141

The 1900s

In the 1900s, sailor suits for boys became simply small versions of a sailor's actual uniform. Children began to wear white sailor suits, with a blue sailor's collar with a white border; under the sailor's jacket they wore a striped jersey in imitation of the sailor's sleeveless waistcoat. They would wear this with dark blue long trousers and a straw hat or a sailor's cap. This was one indication of the increasing bellicosity of Russian society, as was the appearance of military-style overcoats for children aged four and above, normally made out of white cloth with light blue silk embroidered details. Children's overcoats of the 1900s were distinguished by their free cut and their use of fur: for example, beaver fur was used on the collars. Boys aged between twelve and fourteen would wear three-piece suits. A fashion journal wrote: 'Consisting of jacket, trousers and waistcoat, the outfit is normally made from black-and-white chequered material; the jacket is lined with serge, and the sleeves and front part of the waistcoat are lined with bright-coloured satin.'

As had previously been the case, black velvet outfits with lace turndown collars in the musketeer style were very popular. But the most significant new tendency in boy's outfits was the lengthening of trousers for children aged between six and fourteen; to a certain extent this made boys' outfits appear more grown-up, and certainly gave them greater solidity. One further novelty was caps for boys with six or eight folds and a brim that buttoned onto the front.

In the 1900s, knitwear became more and more common for children's clothing, and then went on to be enormously important. Knitted trousers and shirts for children were widespread in Russia, as were knitted shoes for babies. For the first time in many years, sandals were also seen once again. Boys aged between two and four wore short britches with an elastic band at the knee, and a large sewn hem underneath. These were reminiscent of the trousers of an earlier age. Boys aged between ten and twelve wore calf-length white madapolam stockings.

The fashion for low-waisted dresses, often marked by a wide moiré ribbon, continued. However, for girls aged up to four, the fashion was for American-style pleated dresses with banded waists. This fashion gave the child complete freedom of movement and thanks to its practicality, it lasted for approximately a century. For girls aged between ten and fourteen dresses were made with corsages, to emphasise the chest, but with the skirt only extending down to the back of the calf so as to distinguish their fashion from that of their mothers. Colours on the spectrum between dark red and brown were the most fashionable in this period. One novelty was homespun felt hats in the style of the 1830s with black ostrich feather details and taffeta ribbons. In the winter, children covered their feet with high cloth leggings.

As had happened in previous decades, children still enjoyed dressing up and celebrations. Popular were clown costumes, cupids, French hussars, hunters, boyars. In order to help preparation for costume balls, the author Ivchenko published a book, *Themes for Costumes for Masquerades and Tableaux.*

В.Г.Федоровъ, въ Казани.

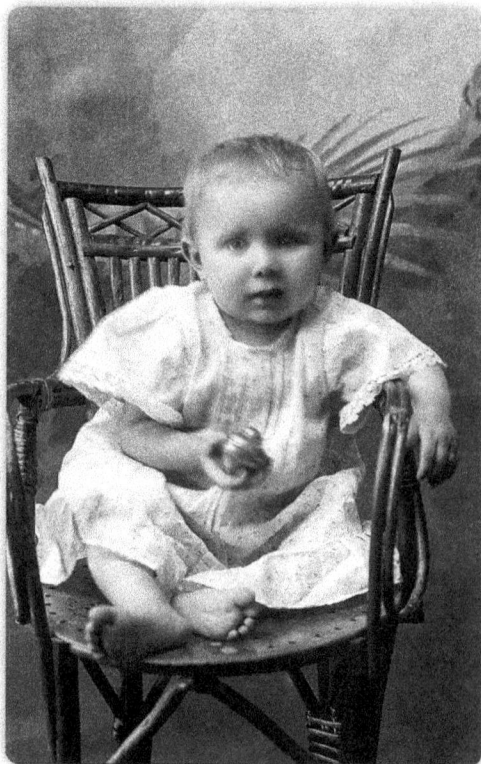

Girl in house dress with upright collar and lace detail. Photograph by V. Fedorov. Kazan. 1900.

Child in house dress with embroidered detail and lace pelerine. Photograph by A. Vasiliev. Samara. 1900.

Child from the Fedorov family in a house dress with lace and embroidered detail. Photograph by I Bakhr. Samara. 1900.

Girl in formal dress with embroidered detail, petticoat and pelerine; on her head a light straw hat. Photograph by V. Aldokhin. Kiev. 1902.

❖ Girl in formal dress in Kate Greenaway style with sewn detail and pelerine. Photograph by A Belyaev. Kazan. 1903.

❖ Sara Rivkin in formal embroidered dress. Photograph by K. Shakhov. Akmolinsk. 1908.

❖ Girl in low-waisted dress with moiré ribbon and upright collar. Saint Petersburg. 1900.

❧ Girl in English-tailored formal dress with a high waist and sewn detail. Photograph by I. Zdobnov. Saint Petersburg. 1900.

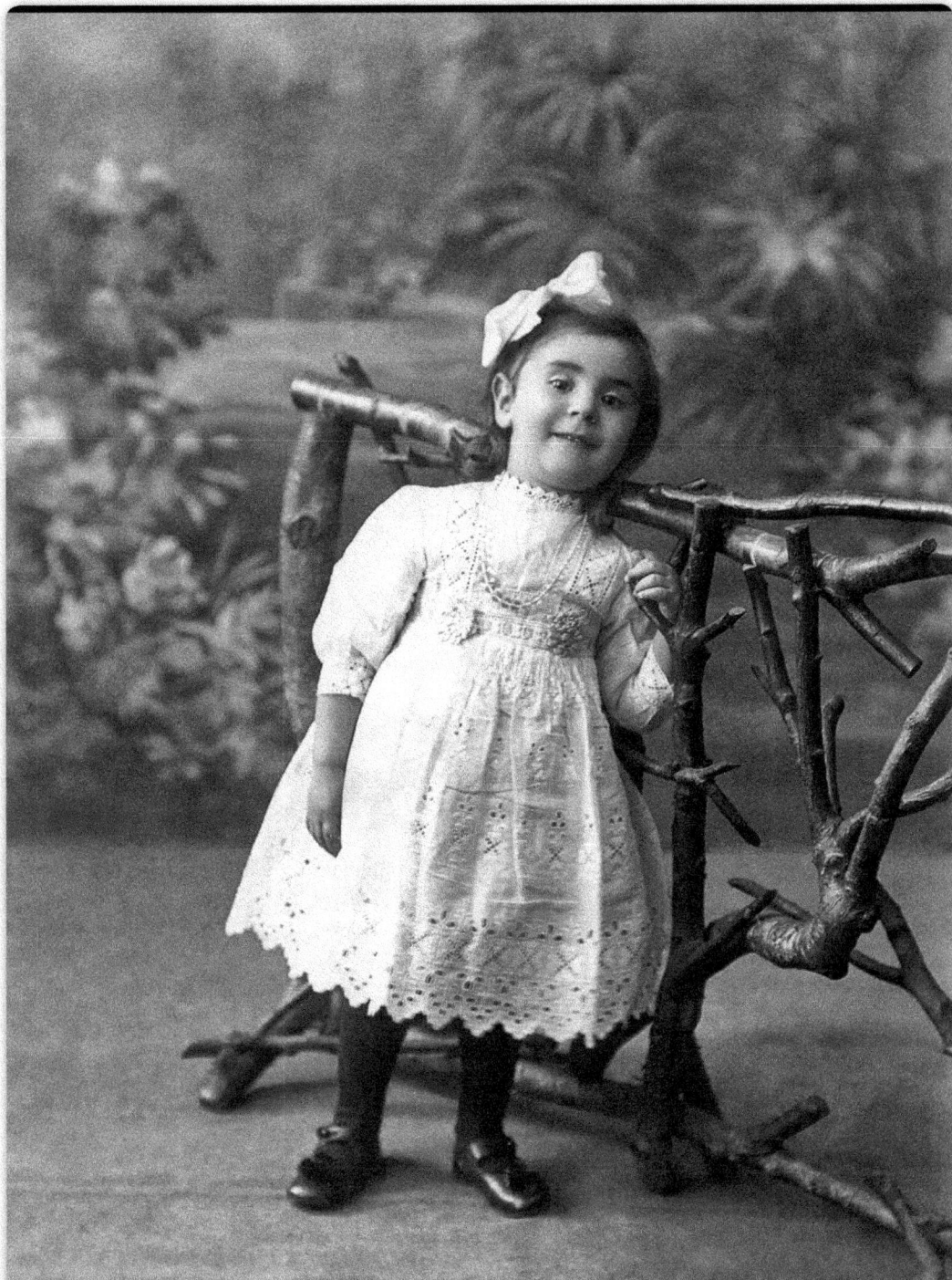

❧ Girl in low-waisted outdoor dress and pelerine, wearing a white fez. Yaroslavl. 1909.

❧ Girl from the Permsky family in formal dress. Photograph by N. Chesnokov. Saint Petersburg. 1900.

❧ Girl in house dress with a pelerine. Photograph by M. Ussakovsky. Tobolsk. 1900.

❧ Brother and sister in house dresses. Russia. 1907.

Girl in house dress with pelerine, lace detail. Photograph by G. Lazovsky. Kiev. 1900.

Girl in formal house dress with turndown collar. Photograph by V. Breitkas. Saint Petersburg. 1900.

Girl in school dress with an apron. Photograph by G. Safontsev. Graivoron. 1900.

Girl in formal dress with lace detail. Russia. 1903.

Girl in expensive formal dress with lace collar. Photograph by V. Vysotsky. Kiev. 1900.

Girls in house dresses with sewn detail and openwork insertions. Moscow. 1900.

Girl in formal house dress with lace detail. Russia. 1900.

Girl in fashionable outdoor outfit: plissé skirt, chequered blouse with silk band at the collar. Photograph by A. Latatuev. Saint Petersburg. 1905.

❧ Girls in sarafans and blouses with upright collars and lace ruche detail. Photograph by A. Gerasimov. Pskov. 1904.

❧ Mila in house dress with embroidered upright collar. Moscow. 1903.

❧ Girl in 'Russian' outfit: blouse and sarafan with artificial pearls, Russian headdress with artificial pearl detail. Photograph by K. Goganson. Petrozavodsk. 1900.

❧ Girl in formal dress with a Vologda lace pelerine. Photograph by D. Antonopulo. Theodosia. 1903.

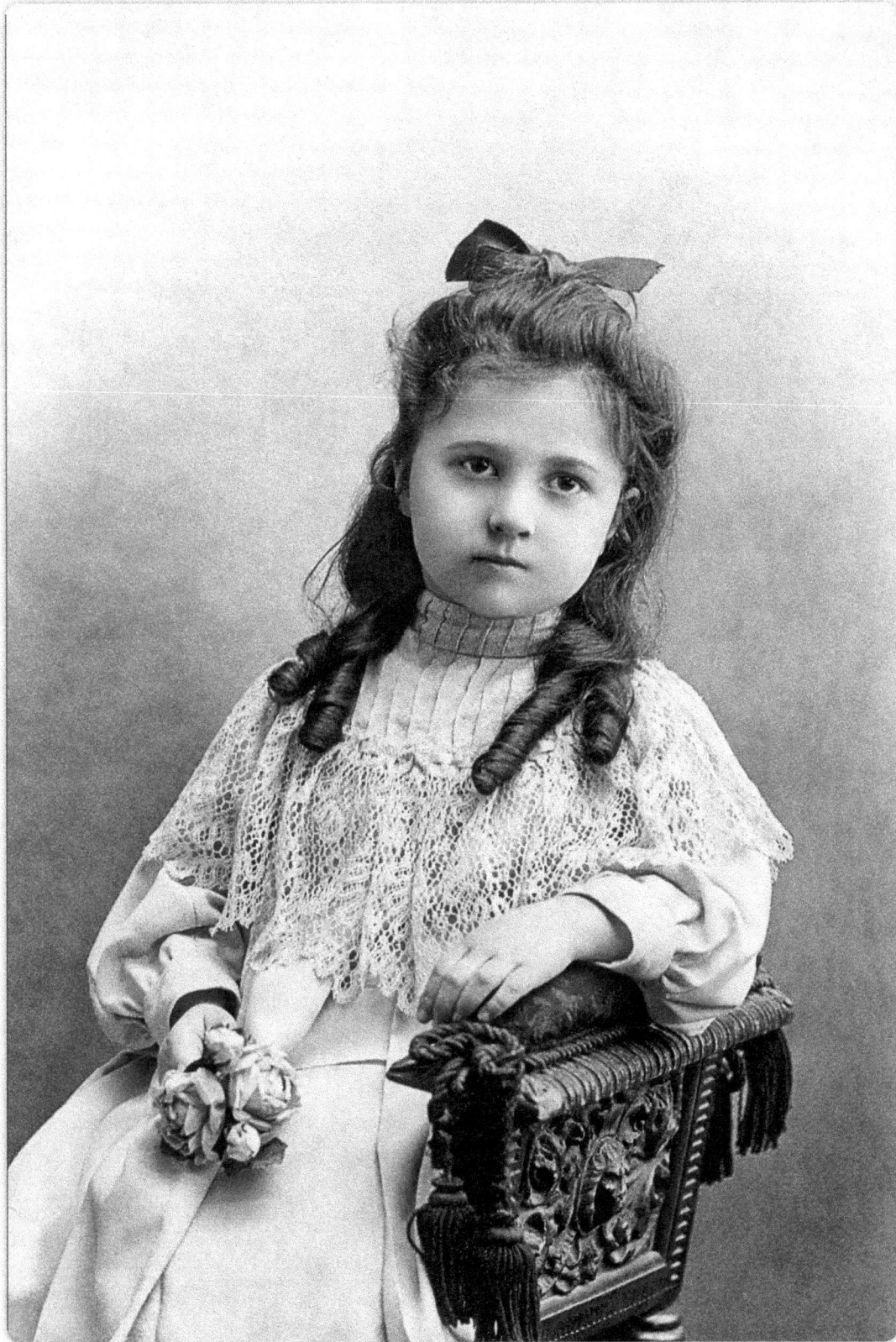

Marusya in black velvet devil costume. Photograph by A. Balaban. Odessa. 1907.

Girl from the Knyazev family in pleated outdoor dress with belt. Russia. 1900.

Marusya in Karaim (Crimean Tatar) national dress. Photograph by A. Balaban. Odessa. 1907.

Girl in school dress with apron and plissé detail. Photograph by P. Polyakov. Uralsk. 1907.

Поляковъ Уральскъ

❧ *Girl in school dress with pelerine and plissé detail. Photograph by M. Dmitriev. Nizhny Novgorod. 1900.*

❧ *Tosya Fadeyeva in house dress with overhanging waist. Helsingfors. 1909.*

❧ *Anya in school dress with plackets. Photograph by V. Ostrovsky. Vitebsk. 1905.*

❧ *Girl in outdoor dress with upright collar and lace detail. Photograph by A. Vainshtain. Odessa. 1903.*

ФОТОГРАФІЯ РУССКАЯ СВѢТОПИСЬ А.ВАЙНШТЕЙНА.

Boy in sailor suit. Vilna. 1900.

Boy from the Fyodorov family in black velvet jacket with a pelerine. Photograph by E. Vasiliev. Samara. 1907.

Boy in house dress with pelerine and sewn detail. Photograph by A. Pazetti. Saint Petersburg. 1900.

Girl in formal dress with turndown collar, wearing hat with satin band and feather. Russia. 1905.

❖ *Petya Terentiev in white woollen outdoor outfit with sailor collar. Photograph by A. Pazetti. Saint Petersburg. 1905.*

❖ *Boy in outdoor outfit: jacket with sailor's collar and short trousers and beret. Photograph by M. Zuev. Harbin. 1906.*

❖ *Boy in sailor suit; taffeta collar, sleeves and trousers. Russia. 1900s.*

❖ *Boy in striped outdoor outfit. Photograph by V. Yegorov. Saint Petersburg. 1906.*

❖ Boy in stylised kosovorotka with embroidered detail, and velvet trousers. Moscow. 1900.

❖ Boy in formal costume. Tiflis. 1906.

❖ Boy in sailor jacket, with decorative anchor, and short narrow trousers. Photograph by R. Sobolev. Saint Petersburg. 1906.

❖ Boy in house dress with lace pelerine. Photograph by V. Fedotova. Russia. 1906.

Boys in fashionable formal outfits with sewn detail. Photograph by A. Yakunin. Perm. 1900.

Boy in Caucasian jacket and white sheepskin papakha. Russia. 1900.

Boy in sailor suit and light straw hat. Photograph by E. Yeggert. Riga. 1905.

Two brothers in outdoor outfits. Photograph by I. Nedeshev. Saint Petersburg. 1900.

"Изящная Свѣтопись" И. Недешева. С. Петербургъ

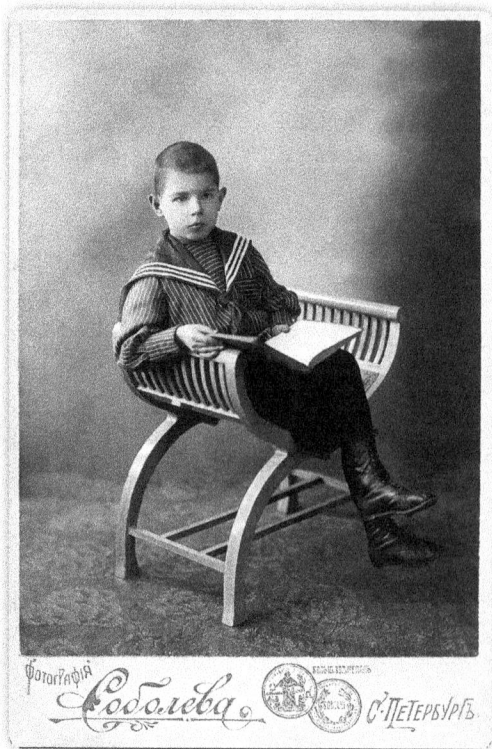

✦ Boy in school uniform. Photograph by
V. Rashtanov. Kiev. 1900.

✦ Boy in formal naval outfit, with white soutache
detail and metal buttons. Photograph by
G. Lazovsky. Kiev. 1900.

✦ Boy in sailor suit. Photograph by R. Sobolev.
Saint Petersburg. 1905.

✦ Boy in fashionable outdoor outfit with
sailor's collar and rep ribbon detail. Tsarskoe
Selo. 1900.

Boys in sailor outfits. Russia. 1900.

Boy in Ukrainian shirt and sheepskin hat. Photograph by I. Danilov. Moscow. 1907.

Gymnazium pupil in uniform. Photograph by M. Gagaev. Nizhny Novgorod. 1900.

Iura Burlakovsky in black velvet formal outfit. Photograph by Mezer. Kiev. 1906.

Brother and sister in formal outfits with sewn detail. Photograph by S. Kanter. Tula. 1904.

Mother and daughter. Girl in striped house dress. Russia. 1901.

Parents with son and daughter. Girl in simple house dress with a pelerine. Boy in shirt with sailor collar and knee britches. Photograph by Fr. Opitz. Moscow. 1904.

Brother and sister in homemade outfits. Photograph by D. Anerik. Saint Petersburg. 1900.

174

◆ Peasant woman with daughter. Girl in high-
waisted sarafan with lace detail and headscarf.
Russia. 1901.

◆ Mother with two daughters. Elder girl in low-
waisted formal dress with ribbon detail and
band fastened at the back. Younger girl in
dress with a pelerine. Russia. 1908.

◆ Brother and sisters. Girls in formal dresses
with frill and lace detail. Boy in formal
costume: jacket with sailor's collar and short
narrow trousers. Photograph by L. Serebrin.
Vilna. 1903.

◆ Brother with two sisters. Girls in homemade
plissé dresses with pleats. Boy in outfit with
sailor collar. Photograph by E. Kalinin. Moscow.
1903.

Mother and father with daughters. Girls in expensive house dresses with sewn detail. Russia. 1906.

Grandmother with grandson. Boy in house dress. Photograph by D. Anerik. Saint Petersburg. 1900.

Nurse with girl. Girl in house dress with a pelerine and sewn detail. Photograph by O. Belinsky. Saint Petersburg. 1900.

Mother and son and daughter. Boy in striped outfit with turndown collar; Girl in house dress with upright collar. Photograph by V. Yegorov. Saint Petersburg. 1906.

Brother and sister. Boy in school shirt with stiff collar, girl in dress with a pelerine. Photograph by B. Butkovska. Vilna. 1903.

Grandmother with grandchildren. Elder girl in low-waisted dress. Younger girl in double-breasted woollen overcoat and knitted hat. Russia. 1900.

Mother with two sons. Boys in kosovorotki. Photograph by Klimenko. Yelets. 1907.

Photographie Artistique

С. Уманскій въ Луганскѣ?

❖ Girl in expensive formal overcoat with a
pelerine with lace detail and a mob cap with
ribbons. Saint Petersburg. 1905.

❖ Boy in jacket with astrakhan detail, and
sheepskin papakha. Photograph by
S. Umansky. Lugansk. 1903.

❖ Girl in plush overcoat with Vologda lace
pelerine and cuffs; hat with Vologda lace
detail and satin ribbon. Photograph by
D. Gershuna. Saint Petersburg. 1906.

❖ Mother with two daughters in winter outfits.
Moscow. C.1905.

Girl in plush winter overcoat. Photograph by Suvorovskaya. Saint Petersburg. 1904.

Group of friends with two girls. Girls in midseason overcoats with false fur pelerines and headdresses. Russia. 1901.

Mother and daughter. Girl in light woollen overcoat with a pelerine and headscarf with ribbon detail. Photograph by A. Latatuev. Saint Petersburg. 1903.

Girl in fashionable overcoat made from ornamented plush and a beret with a feather. Photograph by D. Sakhnovsky. Gatchina. 1903.

184

Misha Ilenko in heavy fur-lined jacket and sheepskin papakha. Photograph by V. Chentsov. Russia. 1908.

Kolya Konshin in winter sheepskin overcoat, white felt boots and white hat. Moscow. 1906.

Boy in double-breasted overcoat and black fur hat. Photograph by V. Leshkov. Russia. 1907.

Mother and son. Boy in sailor outfit with cap. Photograph by F. Kolba. Russia. 1900.

Girl in overcoat with a pelerine and sheepskin collar. Sheepskin hat and muff. Russia. 1908.

Girl in double-breasted overcoat with pelerine. Russia. 1903.

Petya in Caucasian jacket and sheepskin papakha. Photograph by M. Rybakov. Moscow. 1900.

Boy in sheepskin armyaka and 'Russian' hat. Photograph by A. Vishnyakov. Borisoglebsk. 1902.

The 1910s

Between 1910 and 1913 the tendency to make children's clothes versions of adult clothing intensified. Many of the fashions and fabrics which were a part of the adult wardrobe became used for that of children. *Housewives' Journal* noted that 'Nowadays, the laws of fashion allow one to wear more or less anything, including velvet and broché; outfits are no longer divided into clothes for ladies and clothes for younger children, as has heretofore been the case.'

The effect of the First World War was to make economies necessary, and many people were forced to rework and make do with the clothes they had, lengthening skirts and letting in plackets. Protests were made against the very idea of children's fashion in such difficult times — simplicity became the most important factor in the majority of children's clothes. Girls' dresses were low-waisted and knee-length, and simple trapezoidal dresses fastened with a belt and *sarafans* became normal in daily life. The new fashionable fabric became thin cotton flannelette. Small headscarves made of soft flannel became popular. A top-quality purveyor of children's clothing was set up in Petrograd by the purveyors to His Imperial Majesty, the Mersio store on Nevsky Prospect, number 27. Children's shoes were bought from V. Yevstifeyev in Petrograd at Gogol Street, number 12: the shop survived from 1877 until the Revolution. After the popular Revolution, the commercialisation of children's clothing in Russia changed drastically — just as life in general did. The nationalisation of industry, and in particular that of the fabric industry, led to an actual lack of textiles and a decline in the manufacture of clothing. The lack of fabric and premade children's clothing led to parents being regularly forced to concoct children's clothing out of adult's clothes, for example, making girls' *sarafans* out of an old overcoat. The wide spread of knitted clothes was due to their relative cheapness and comfort. The silhouette of dresses for young girls had a great influence on what would be the cut of clothes for adults women after the First World War. The most popular model was the straight-cut low-waisted dress, similar to those Paul Poiret was making for his daughters as early as 1911. Girls' dresses were made of thin cotton fabric printed with constructivist patterns, including symbols from the early Soviet period. These sleeveless dresses were worn with white stockings and flat 'Pinet' sandals (named after the French shoe manufacturer Pinet), which were considered the height of luxury.

The long-standing sailor-style dress for girls, which had been in fashion for more or less forty years, fell into disuse, as it was considered a hangover from the past. However, sailor suits for boys, often worn with white stockings, remained popular.

A great problem was posed by winter clothing for boys — they were ashamed of their old regime fur coats and no longer wore the rabbit or marten that they had used in the previous decade. The fur linings from gentlemen's overcoats, leftovers from the previous regime, were often deployed.

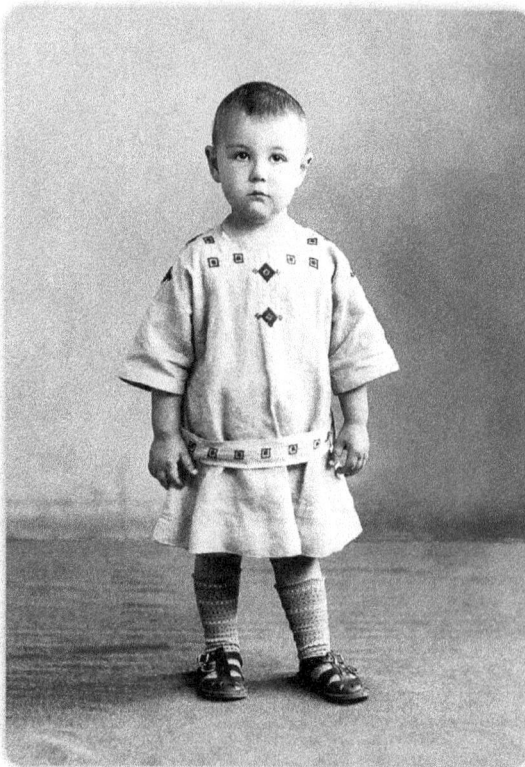

Girl in house formal dress with sewn detail and lace attachment. Alma-Ata. 1913.

Girl in low-waisted dress with lace collar. Saratov. 1914.

Girl in simple low-waisted house dress with embroidered detail. Photograph by E. Semenenko. Saint Petersburg. 1910.

Verochka Mikhaleva in formal dress with lace detail and decorative silk ribbons. Kharkov. 1912.

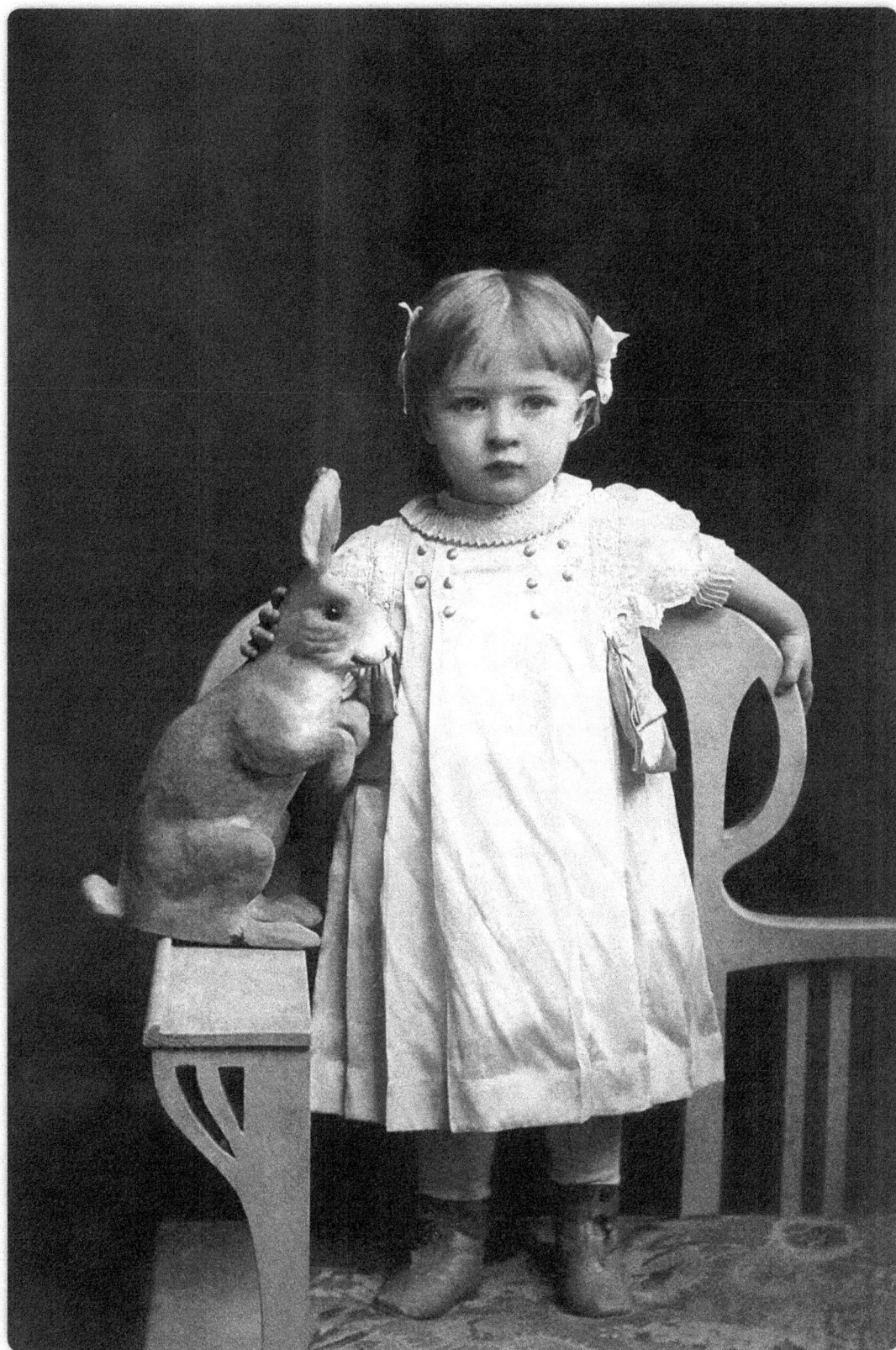

❖ Girl in house dress with an apron. Saint Petersburg. 1910.

❖ Girl in dark velvet dress with a pelerine. Russia. 1910.

Girl in sailor style dress. Russia. 1915.

❖ Girl in striped dress with lace pelerine. Russia. 1914.

Girl in house dress with light straw hat. Russia. C.1911.

Girl in folk outfit. Russia. 1910.

Girl in low-waisted dress with plackets, decorated with embroidered butterflies.. Photograph by R. Sobolev. Saint Petersburg. 1912.

Shura Yakovleva in formal lace dress. Moscow. 1910.

CABINET PORTRAIT

Sonya in simple cotton house dress.
Photograph by N. Lepsky. Yekaterinoslav. 1914.

Girl in formal lace dress with silk ribbon
detail. Russia. 1915.

Antonina Morozova in style moderne
overcoat with leg-of-mutton sleeves and
decorative buttons. Photograph by Ziskind.
Bryansk. 1910.

Boy in sailor suit. Photograph by
M. Seliverstov. Voronezh. 1912.

❧ *Boy in stylised kosovorotka. Photograph by K. Zoganson. Petrozavodsk. 1910.*

❧ *Boy in white woollen house outfit. Photograph by I. Varenik. Orel. 1912.*

❧ *Koka in sailor suit. Photograph by T. Lubitsch. Saint Petersburg. 1911.*

Kolya and Vladik in sailor outfits. Russia. 1910.

Boy in sailor suit. Photograph by K. Zoganson. Petrozavodsk. 1911.

Boy in velvet jacket. Photograph by V. Seliverstov. Voronezh. 1912.

Two brothers in trousers and shirts with ties. Photograph by V.I. Borisov. Russia. 1915.

Three brothers in home outfits. Samara. 1910.

Boy in sailor suit. Photograph by V. Zatorsky. Kovno. 1913.

Boy in summer outdoor outfit: double-breasted jacket with turndown collar and short trousers, and light straw hat. Russia. 1910.

Boy in woollen sukmana. Tomsk. 1917.

Alexander Poluboyarinov in double-breasted woollen overcoat, English cap, holding a walking stick. Moscow. 1912.

Gymnazium pupil in uniform. Photograph by O.Renar. Moscow. 1910.

Mother with son and daughter, dressed in school uniform. Photograph by M. Sorokin. Arkhangelsk. 1916.

М. Сорокинъ г. Архангельскъ

❖ *Shatalov family with their daughter. Girl in outdoor dress with rep ribbon detail on the collar and cuffs. Kharkov. 1911.*

❖ *Sister with brothers in sailor outfits. Photograph by G. Vesenberg. Petrograd. 1915.*

❖ *Brother and sister. Girl in sailor suit with inkle detail on the collar and cuffs. Boy in formal costume: jacket with sailor collar, short trousers. Russia. 1915.*

❖ *Boys in sailor outfits. Girls in formal dresses with lace detail. Russia. 1910.*

❖ Bessarabian family. Boy in summer outfit with sailor collar. Photograph by K. Lapin. Izmail. 1913.

❖ Two boys. One in thin cotton kosovorotka and short black velvet trousers; the other in thin cotton suit. Russia. 1915.

❖ Brother and sister. Girl in low-waisted house dress with lace collar; Boy in striped blouse and short trousers. Russia. 1915.

❖ The actress Mura Chuloshnikova with Kirochka. Girl in formal dress with lace collar and lace mob cap. Russia. 1913.

❖ Two brothers and sister. Boys in school uniform. Girl in white summer outfit. Russia. 1912.

❖ Grandfather with granddaughter. Girl in dark velvet dress with turndown collar. Kiev. 1916.

❖ Father and daughter. Girl in house dress with lace detail. Russia. 1910.

❖ Mother and daughter. Girl in formal dress with velvet ribbon detail on collar, cuffs and hem. Photograph by G. Mukhin. Slavyansk. 1911.

✤ *Mother and son. Boy in riding outfit. Kharkov. 1913.*

✤ *The Elyashberg family. Boy in woollen outfit: jacket with sailor's collar and short trousers. Girl in dress with a pelerine and upright collar. Russia. 1910.*

✤ *A.K. and E.N. Ratkov with their children Valya and Rita, in house dresses with sailor collars. Kostroma. 1915.*

✤ *Mother and daughter. Girl in formal dress with lace detail. Kiev. 1916.*

♦ Mother with her daughter Lida and her son Vitya. Lida in low-waisted house dress. Vitya in dark woollen outfit. Photograph by B. Mischenko. Rostov. 1915.

♦ Girl in overcoat and hat decorated with flowers. Photograph by M. Sorokin. Arkhangelsk. 1916.

♦ Mother and son. Boy in Russian-style outfit: stylised kosovorotka and light velvet trousers. Samara. 1913.

✤ Boy in double-breasted winter overcoat with sheepskin collar and 'Russian' hat. Photograph by A. Vasiliev. Russia. 1914.

✤ Zhenya in artificial wool coat, little hat and muff. Russia. 1913.

Girl in double-breasted sheepskin overcoat. Photograph by A. Ivanitsky. Kharkov. 1910.

✤ Sisters in fashionable double-breasted overcoats with a pelerine and plissé detail and sheepskin hats. Photograph by I. Erdman. Tsaritsyn. 1912.

❖ Girl in winter overcoat with a pelerine and cuffs with fur detail, and a fur hat. Russia. 1915.

❖ Girl in overcoat and hat. Russia. 1910.

❖ Boy in sheepskin armyaka and hat. Russia. 1917.

❖ Father with two daughters. Girls in overcoats and hats made from artificial fur. Photograph by N. Tarasov. Kozlov. 1914.

❖ Two brothers and sister. Boys in woollen overcoats and caps; girl in overcoat with a pelerine, rep ribbon detail, hat and muff made from artificial fur. Russia. 1914.

Mother and son. Boy in woollen outfit and hat. Russia. 1914.

Mother and daughter. Girl in double-breasted plush overcoat and hat tied on with a kerchief. Russia. 1913.

Glagoslav Publications Catalogue

- *The Time of Women* by Elena Chizhova
- *Sin* by Zakhar Prilepin
- *Hardly Ever Otherwise* by Maria Matios
- *The Lost Button* by Irene Rozdobudko
- *Khatyn* by Ales Adamovich
- *Christened with Crosses* by Eduard Kochergin
- *The Vital Needs of the Dead* by Igor Sakhnovsky
- *METRO 2033* (Dutch Edition) by Dmitry Glukhovsky
- *METRO 2034* (Dutch Edition) by Dmitry Glukhovsky
- *A Poet and Bin Laden* by Hamid Ismailov
- *A Russian Story* by Eugenia Kononenko
- *Kobzar* by Taras Shevchenko
- *White Shanghai* by Elvira Baryakina
- *The Stone Bridge* by Alexander Terekhov
- *King Stakh's Wild Hunt* by Uladzimir Karatkevich
- *Depeche Mode* by Serhii Zhadan
- *Wolf Messing – The True Story of Russia`s Greatest Psychic* by Tatiana Lungin
- *Herstories*, An Anthology of New Ukrainian Women Prose Writers
- *Watching The Russians* (Dutch Edition) by Maria Konyukova
- *A Book Without Photographs* by Sergei Shargunov
- *The Grand Slam and Other Stories* (Dutch Edition) by Leonid Andreev
- *The Battle of the Sexes Russian Style* by Nadezhda Ptushkina
- *Down Among The Fishes* by Natalka Babina
- *disUNITY* by Anatoly Kudryavitsky
- *Sankya* by Zakhar Prilepin
- *Andrei Tarkovsky – A Life on the Cross* by Lyudmila Boyadzhieva
- *Solar Plexus* by Rustam Ibragimbekov
- *Don't Call me a Victim!* by Dina Yafasova
- *Tsarina Alexandra's Diary* (Dutch)

More coming soon...

www.ingramcontent.com/pod-product-compliance
Lightning Source LLC
Chambersburg PA
CBHW080358030426
42334CB00024B/2917